Easy Camping Meal Plans

Recipes and Shopping Lists for 2, 3 or 5-Day Camping Trips

Louise Davidson

ISBN: 9781699589373

Printed in the United States

www.thecookbookpublisher.com

CONTENTS

INTRODUCTION

Hello, campers! Welcome to our new camping cookbook.

We've provided a selection of complete recipe menus for 2-, 3-, and 5-day camping trips, for a family (or group) of four. Each menu has been carefully planned to minimize the different foods and equipment you need to bring, but also to avoid seeming to serve the same meals over and over. We don't want to sacrifice variety! The result is a selection of meal plans that conveniently use the same ingredients but are but not repetitive.

In these pages you won't find a single hot dog or hamburger, so you can go ahead and leave the ketchup and relish at home. (You might need a little bit of mustard, though.) **Almost all of our meals are made in one pot** – and many without any pot at all!

We are also excited to present a shopping list for each menu, including the amounts of each thing you'll need. It's that easy! But please note that our Shopping list does not include snacks and drinks – you'll need to add those. Also, you may occasionally have half an onion left over. C'est la vie.

In our quest for efficiency, we've incorporated some tips and tricks we know you're going to love. We'll show you a few ways to save on time and effort; like preparing extra meats and grains ahead of time. We'll even show you a few ways to turn a bit of casserole into a completely different meal. Leftovers? Where?

There are three sections:

Healthy Menus

Our collection of healthy menus focuses on whole foods and lean fats. If you want to focus on nutrition for your campers, this selection is for you. With recipes like <u>Almond Chicken</u>, <u>Pineapple Turkey Skewers</u>, and <u>Coconut Coffee Cake</u>, you'll never get bored.

No-Fuss Menus

If you'd like to leave the fuss and bother at home and let loose on your camping trip, then come have some fun with us! We haven't completely thrown nutrition to the wind – you'll find plenty of fresh fruit and vegetables and "real foods" like <u>Roast Pork Dinner</u> and <u>Chicken Pot Pie</u> – but we've used some convenience foods (like premade biscuit dough and bagged vegetables) so you can minimize your cooking effort and eat deliciously well at the same time.

Vegetarian Menus

If you follow a vegetarian diet, we have you covered. Our vegetarian section includes a selection of whole grains, lentils, beans, and a wide variety of fresh vegetables. If you have a non-vegetarian coming along on the trip, don't worry – we have recipes using normal foods that everyone will enjoy, such as <u>Black Bean Lasagna</u> and <u>Orange Pistachio Brown Rice.</u>

So, no matter your tastes or habits, we know you're going to love this cookbook as much as we do.

Before jumping into the menus and recipes, in the following chapters, we cover some important information about cooking in the great outdoors, including food prep and safety, cooking equipment and utensils, a list of essentials to bring on a camping trip, tips on planning ahead, being environmentally friendly when camping, and practical camping food hacks. Then we get in the meat of thing sort of speaking with the camping cooking methods: foil packets, grilling over the barbecue or camping stove, Dutch oven cooking, and campfire cooking.

One last thing before we get started, if you would like to **print the shopping lists**, you can do so by by visiting my publisher's website www.thecookbookpublisher.com and you will find the pdf document under the Authors' tab on my page - Louise Davidson.

FOOD PREP AND SAFETY

Of course, there is nothing magical about getting sick after noshing on food that's been tainted. Not only does it ruin your trip, but if you're in the back country, it's going to be awhile before you can get to a doctor.

So, let's eliminate the possibility of even coming close to contaminating your food by going over some simple precautions you can take that will ensure you have the best trip ever.

Packing for Camping

Use a hard-shelled cooler instead of insulated bags for long camping trips. These are much better at keeping groceries cool and will ensure you get mileage out of the food you take.

It is best to store your raw meats in their own cooler. In fact, it is not just best, it should be the rule.

Use leak-proof containers or mason jars when you pack your food.

If you've cooked something to take on your trip, cool it, and transport it cold to prevent bad bacteria from forming.

It is important that you pack your foodstuffs correctly to ensure that they stay cold and don't get contaminated. With that in mind, if for any reason you need to pack your raw meats and other foodstuffs together, pack your raw stuff on the bottom so there is no danger of contaminated liquids leaking over other food.

After you've filled your cooler, you're done with foods that have to be refrigerated. Now move on to things that will stay safe in warmer temperatures including:

Nuts and dried fruit
Nut butters
Canned fish and meats
Dried meats
Fruit drinks
Pasta, rice, noodles

Definitely pack a food thermometer so you can ensure your meats are cooked all the way through. Please see the internal temperature cooking charts in the appendix at the end of the book.

Food Safety and Cooking Guidelines

Whenever you are cooking away from home, extra precautions are needed when it comes to safety. Pay close attention or you can turn a wonderful camping trip into an unpleasant one. To avoid this, follow the appropriate procedure.

The most important thing to keep in mind is the temperature of your food. Perishable foods must be kept at a temperature below 40°F. Make sure to bring a cooler to keep your food safe, and bring a thermometer to check the temperature. If you notice that the temperature is over 40°F, throw the food away. Don't ever try to keep or salvage any food that has been sitting out of its safe zone.

Always double wrap your meat in a plastic bag and keep it tightly closed. Keep raw meat and poultry separate from the other items. Bring a meat thermometer, as it will enable you to check the internal temperature of meat before you consume it. The internal temperature of 165°F is ideal for ground meat and poultry. Beef has a bigger range of acceptable temperatures, which can vary from 145°F (medium-rare) to 170°F (well cooked). Always make sure to follow these guidelines. The same goes for any ingredients that come in contact with raw meat, which is something that happens in the foil packets.

The next thing you want to check is just how hot your source of heat is. Outdoor heat sources are not always predictable, which is why you may need to modify the cooking time listed in a recipe. The majority of recipes here will require a heat source with the medium-high temperature of around 400°F.

If you have any leftovers, wrap them and cool them immediately. Don't let them sit for long because they can quickly become contaminated.

Finally…be careful not to burn yourself. When you open a hot foil packet, steam is released and it rises upwards. Always use tongs to remove the packet from the source of heat and then cut a small slit in a shape of an "X" into the packet. This will release the steam.

Safe Food Handling Tips

Be mindful of safe food-handling practices. Keep meats and dairy products well wrapped, chilled, and away from other foods. Also, it's best to pack your cooler with frozen meat, which will help cool the other items and keep it fresh for a few days. Here are some other pointers:

- Make sure you wash your hands with soap and water after handling raw meat.

- Remember to wash any utensils that contact with raw meat as well to prevent cross-contamination.

- Make sure you don't have leaky raw meat packages lying around that contaminate other things.

- If you have hot leftovers, let them cool, and store them in a cold place as quickly as possible.

- If prepared food has sat out in the sun for more than an hour, toss it.

- Do not leave foodstuffs out. Not only do you risk contamination but you can also attract animals to your site.

- Never leave a campfire unattended, especially if children are around.

- Make sure any pots, grills, or grates are secure and will not tip when they're loaded with hot food.

- No gas! Don't spray any accelerants into your cooking fire.

- When you're done, make sure the fire is completely out.

- At night, store your cooler and other food containers in your vehicle if possible. Plastic bins with locking lids are a good choice for storing food that doesn't need to be cold. And remember, animals that find food around your site will definitely be back for more, and they are crafty.

Cooking Equipment and Utensils

Aside from basic essentials like a few pots and pans, a large wooden spoon, a chef's knife and cutting board, and knives, forks, spoons, cups, bowls and plates for serving, there are some particularly useful items that are worth mentioning here.

Aluminum foil: you may not even need to bring any other cookware, because you can cook a meal, a snack and even dessert by wrapping ingredients in foil and cooking over the campfire, a grill, or hot coals. Foil is also a life saver when you're wary of cooking on the rusty-looking grill at the campsite or other questionable surfaces. Double your layers to avoid tearing, or use heavy-duty foil.

Briquettes: compressed charcoal and other materials which are lit and allowed to heat up for cooking with a grill or Dutch oven. There are self-lighting briquettes that already contain lighter fluid and are easy to light, but they give off an unpleasant odor. Regular charcoal briquettes may take a little more time to get going, but they help lend a smoky flavor to food.

Cast iron skillet: its versatility allows you to use it for dishes from breakfast hash to steaks to cakes. Cast iron distributes heat well and so is ideal for cooking over charcoal or firewood. A well-seasoned skillet can be just as good, if not better, than a nonstick pan. A small selection of these would be nice, but they are heavy to carry. If you're hiking to your campsite, you'll want to choose one that is lighter. Go with a 12"–14" model, preferably one with a lid (though foil will do).

Charcoal or Gas Grill: parks and campsites usually provide grills, but you may not be comfortable using their rusty-looking grates. Veteran campers recommend lining suspicious-looking grates with aluminum foil to be safe, but you could just bring your own portable grill. A metal grill with legs that fold will be a huge help at the campsite. You can cook food directly on the grate, use foil packets, or place your skillet on it.

Camping stove: if you want, but not absolutely necessary, it's practical to have on hand a camping stove. It usually has 1 or 2 burners and often is wind safe. They usually use propane as fuel. These are nice to have in when you don't necessarily want to wait to built a fire or light up some charcoal or you need more reliable cooking temperature. It's very handy when you need coffee first thing in the morning!

Dutch oven: a Dutch oven just might be your best friend during your trip. It can easily serve as a makeshift oven for preparing favorites like pot roasts, stews, pasta dishes, breads, and cakes. Campers usually use an outdoor Dutch oven with legs which make it ideal for cooking over coals. The shape of the lid allows you to place coals on top, too. Usually, the Dutch oven is placed on top of a ring of coals or briquettes. The rule is "diameter in inches minus three" for the bottom and "diameter in inches plus three," for the top. In other words, if your Dutch oven has a 10-inch diameter, you would use a ring of 7 briquettes underneath and 13 briquettes on top.

Barbecue skewers: metal skewers are very useful at camp, as they can be used to cook a variety of foods; marshmallows and hot dogs being only the beginning. For roasting over the campfire, you'll want longer ones so you can sit away from the flames. You might also choose to purchase some of the shorter variety for cooking on a grill. This type should have no plastic or wooden handles, because those won't stand up to the heat.

Hobo Pie Maker: an ingenious contraption that makes it easy and fun to prepare sandwiches and even desserts on the campfire.

Meat thermometer: even the most experienced cooks can have a hard time knowing when a meat dish is done. A thermometer will make it easier for you to determine when the meat is ready – and eliminate the risk of your trip being ruined by food poisoning from improperly-cooked meat.

Nonstick cooking spray: not only is it convenient to use, but it can also mean a few less calories in the dish.

Ziploc bags: convenient and space saving. You can use them for storing precooked pasta, marinades, herbs, spices, cut-up veggies, and almost anything you can think of. This will help simplify and organize your cooking.
.

Aluminum baking pans and trays: these disposable pans are very useful for various things at the campsite, so it's good to have some on hand. They're available in many sizes and shapes. Consult your meal plan so you can be sure you haven't overlooked the kind you need.

Oven Mitts: silicon oven mitts are heat-resistant and won't give you a nasty burn if they're wet. They're also easier to clean than the mitts you use at home.

Tongs: be sure to bring a sturdy set of long metal tongs, for moving foil packets around in the coals.

Mason jars: these are great to mix dressings, store trail mix, cereals, and batters, and be used for many other things.

SOME ESSENTIALS TO BRING ON YOUR TRIP

Here is a quick check list of thing you might want to bring according to their purpose:

For the fire
- Waterproof matches or a few good lighters
- Starter liquid fluid
- Starter wood
- Charcoals (plenty of it)
- Cooking utensils for barbecue: tongs, spatula, extra-long forks, cleaning brush for the grill.
- Grill (for over the fire, if the campsite does not provide or you like having your own)
- A grate to place directly on the fire to cook food on the open flame

To prepare and cook the food
- Large cast iron skillet or metal skillet that can be placed on the grill or fire
- Saucepan
- Heavy-duty aluminum foil
- Cooking spray of your choice.
- Olive oil, butter
- Salt and pepper and other seasoning you may want to use, like garlic powder, chili powder, and other spices.
- Oven mitts (preferably silicone to accommodate very high temperatures)
- Can opener
- Bottle opener
- Prepping knifes, cutting board
- Whisk, spoons, wooden spoon, slotted spoon
- Grater, vegetable peeler
- Plastic strainer

- Large unbreakable serving plates
- Mixing bowl, various size
- Measuring cups and spoons
- Wood skewers
- Zip lock bags
- Mason jars

To keep the food
- One cooler with plenty of ice or ice packs to keep perishable food and drinks fresh
- A second cooler or large plastic covered bin for dry non-perishable item like cans, pasta, rice, cereals, seasoning & spices.
- Plastic wrap
- Plastic airtight containers for food leftover storage

To eat
- Non-breakable plates, glass, cups, mugs, utensils
- Napkins
- Plastic tablecloth
- Water bottles

To clean-up
- Paper towels
- Washing clothes, drying clothes
- Dishwashing tub, dishwashing soap

PLAN AHEAD!

A meal plan is an absolute must when you're camping. Presumably, you'll be away from a grocery store, so you'll need to pack enough servings of each food to satisfy everyone.

Not only do you need to know what foods to pack, planning *how* you're going to prepare the food gives you the opportunity to take along needed items, like foil baking pans.

You can make cooking at the campsite even easier on yourself by doing some of the food prep at home. Plastic food storage bags with secure closures are great for carrying premade ingredients in. They can be washable or disposable depending on your preference, they can easily be labeled, and they are the most compact way of storing food in small spaces.

When preparing food at home for the campsite, you have a couple of different options. With some dishes, you can prepare all of the ingredients and combine them together in one container so that all you need to do is transfer them from the container they will be cooked in. If you find that many of the dishes that you plan on preparing use the same ingredients, you can prepare larger quantities of those ingredients and store them in a plastic bag, retrieving only what you need at any given time. You can also prepare each set of ingredients for dishes separately, bag and label it, and then assemble it at the campsite. For instance, planning a cake recipe, you can prepare the dry ingredients at home and add the wet ingredient at the campsite and in some cases the whole batter and freeze it until you need it.

When camping, you don't have to give up homemade flavor in favor of convenience foods. However certain premade, canned, and frozen foods not only save you time, but can also be easily enhanced with just a few small additions. For example, a jarred

13

sauce with the addition of a few spices will taste heavenly and save you the extra time and ingredients of creating it from scratch.

Always pack a little extra. You never know when you will want seconds or meet a new mouth to feed. Welcome others into your campsite and make new friends and memories around the campfire enjoying a homemade dessert.

BE ENVIRONMENTALLY FRIENDLY

When you're enjoying the outdoors, don't forget to leave it as unchanged as possible after your visit. Campgrounds have facilities for toileting and waste management, so use common sense and be mindful of any recycling requests.

When you're camping in the wild, it's even more important not to leave evidence of your cooking behind.

When possible, leave wrappers at home. Some things (like meats and pre-made salads) can be better packed and stored in reusable containers to avoid seepage and crushing. Leaving those boxes and bags at home means you won't have to deal with them at the campsite. Once the containers are empty, you can use them to take garbage (like soiled plastic wrappers) back home for proper disposal.

You can burn napkins, paper towels, paper plates, carboard, tissues, and bones, but avoid putting any foam or plastic in the fire. This releases harmful toxins that you shouldn't breathe, and that are hard on the environment.

Use separate bags for garbage and recycling, and make sure none of your trash is left around on the ground.

CAMPING FOOD HACKS

So part of the fun of cooking in the great outdoors is getting inventive. If you're a frequent camper, then you've definitely had to fashion cutlery or utensils out of some very strange things at one point or another.

Check out some of the following camp food hacks you can try out on your next camping trip:

- **Bread:** Instead of having your bread squished up among all the other things you're taking with you camping, keep it in a large, clean, tin can. Open it up at the site and enjoy non-squished-bread sandwiches. You can use any recipe you like for the baking of the bread.

- **Water:** Freeze your water supply in large containers that you can place inside your cooler. They will keep the cooler cold and can be used for drinking water later.

- **Tortillas:** as an alternative to bread, take tortilla flour wraps. They take up less space than bread and can be used to make wraps, thin pizzas, and can even be crisped up for some chip-like action with salsa.

- **Take salsa!** Salsa is so versatile and will bring a new layer of flavor to your camping meals. It can be used in a ton of ways including as a dip, pasta sauce, in a stew, on tacos, on hot dogs – the choices are endless.

- **Spices and herbs:** cooking meats and veggies with your basic salt and black pepper is alright if you're camping for just a day or two, but if you plan on trying out the recipes in this book, you will want to take along some other spices. A great way to make your spices portable is to store small amounts in Tic-Tac boxes.

- **Fire starters:** If you live somewhere where you can get some birch bark, grab some of that easy-burning fuel, bag it, and take it with you for starting campfires in a flash.

- **DIY grill:** you can make a portable grill with an aluminum tray filled with hot coals with a rack placed on top.

- **Burgers:** when cooking burgers over a fire, place an ice cube on each burger and you will avoid drying out the inside of the burger.

- **Aluminum foil** is the best way to pack food, because you can cook it over the fire during camping. Do remember to bring lots with you!

- **Omelets:** you can make an omelet by boiling it in a Ziploc® bag until the eggs are set.

- **Bacon and sausages**: precooking bacon or sausages at home saves a lot of time and mess at the campsite.

- **Batters:** before leaving home, clean empty condiment bottles and fill them with pancake batter, cake batter, or premixed omelets to take along with you for an easy meal.

- **Ice**: fill large, sturdy, resealable bags with water, and freeze these (flat) ahead of time. They are easier than ice cubes to pack in the cooler, they take longer to thaw, and then they become safe drinking water!

- **Eggs:** consider cracking your eggs into a bottle and transporting them that way instead of in the shell. They'll be scrambled, but they are much tidier and easier to pack this way! One water bottle will hold 6–8 eggs.

- **Refrigerated dough:** whether you make it yourself or buy the rolls from the fridge at the grocery store, prepared dough (for croissants, biscuits, and cinnamon rolls) saves you a lot of time and effort at the campsite. It's very versatile and can be cooked in a number of different ways.

- **Milk alternatives**: we use milk for so many things, but it can be a challenge to handle safely at the campsite. Pack powdered and canned milk for emergencies; it can be used in coffee and some recipes. Also, milk can be purchased in Tetra Paks, which keep for months with no refrigeration. They're not always easy to find, but they do make life easier when there's no fridge nearby.

- **Bacon:** precook your bacon to about three-quarters done at home, and store it in a lidded plastic container with a sheet or two of paper towel. This saves you a lot of greasy mess at mealtime, and it will already have shrunk so you'll fit more into the same space. MORE BACON!

- **Canned whipped cream:** nothing dresses up a dessert more than a little squirt of pressurized whipped cream. Grab a few cans to keep in the cooler for desserts you'll all remember.

CAMPING COOKING METHODS

In this cookbook, you will find that most recipes use one of the four basic camping cooking methods. These are:

1) Foil packets

Foil packet is a great cooking method for cooking outdoors. You only need to place your ingredients on a foil sheet, fold, seal, and cook to enjoy a quick and mess-free meal.

2) Grilling / Camping stove

Grilling is the most known cooking method for the outdoors. You just grill your meat, fish, and other ingredients until perfectly cooked and charred to your liking. You can do this on the barbecue grill over a charcoal or campfire heat source or you can use a camping stove which is usually fueled with propane.

3) Cast Iron Dutch Oven

Cooking food in a cast iron Dutch oven is one of the easiest ways to cook during a camping trip as you do not need to check the state of the food all the time but just take care of the heat source, it being the campfire, charcoal or wood fire, propane stove, etc. The flavors develop over time and you can feed an army with one pot meals!

4) Campfire cooking

Basically, campfire cooking is using the campsite fire to cook your food directly over the flame.

FOIL PACKETS

The best thing about foil packet cooking is that it is extremely easy. You will quickly master all the techniques needed and you will use minimal tools in the process. Here are some of the basic things you need to know when it comes to preparing a foil packet meal for your campsite.

What You Need

Usually, a heat source, cooking spray, aluminum foil, and some food are everything you need. Nothing more. **Always pick heavy-duty aluminum foil as this is better for foil packet cooking.** You need to fold it, and heavy-duty foil will hold up much better, and it is much handier to use it when you move your packet to the source of heat. This type of foil keeps all crimps and folds you made and you will be sure that all the steam and juices are held in the foil. It also comes in many width sizes. Depending on your family, pick one that will suit your needs.

Heat Sources

Any heat source will serve well for foil packet cooking, so you can use a grill, fire pit or propane source of heat. What you need to make sure of is not to place the foil packets you make directly on the flame. When using a fire pit or a grill, you want to prepare it by setting fire to some coals or wood. Let the fire burn down until the coals or wood are really hot but without an open flame. Arrange the packets to cook so they are a few inches away from the heat source, and turn them occasionally for even cooking.

Cooking Sprays and Fats

Always make sure to spray the foil with cooking spray. You don't want your food to stick to the foil or get charred. The only situation when you can skip this step is if the food you are preparing already has enough oil to provide an adequate protective coating. Alternatives to cooking spray include melted butter or cooking oil; a light brushing of either of these is equally effective.

Feel Free to Experiment, But Keep Your Ingredients in Mind

When you start discovering the endless possibilities foil packet cooking offers, you will want to make your own packets. You should definitely try this, so feel free to experiment! There is one thing to keep in mind here, and that is the size and type of the ingredients you want to mix. For example, thin pieces of meat can only be combined with thinly sliced vegetables. You see, hard vegetables need longer cooking times, so if you mix them with thinly sliced meat, you will end up either undercooking the vegetables or overcooking the meat, simply because you put them both in one foil packet.

Always think of the cooking process when you choose your ingredients. Other good advice is to have at least one ingredient with a certain level of moisture, especially if the recipe you are creating is rather dry. In foil packet cooking, it's a tricky thing to add the ingredients once the cooking process has begun. This is why you need to be sure that you have made the right combination before you start. Tomatoes, marinades, and butter are examples of ingredients with moisture you can use.

Assembly

When you prepare your packets, keep in mind the variable cooking times for the ingredients you are using. The ingredients that need to be cooked the longest should be placed at the bottom of the foil, so they will have the most exposure to the source of heat.
Let's take an example. If you're combining meat with vegetables, a good choice is to put the meat to the bottom of the foil and then top it with vegetables, because meat demands longer cooking time. Another thing to note is the blending and texture of the ingredients you use. When you have an ingredient that will melt, like cheese, then put it nearest to the ingredient you want to mix it with so you can get the best flavor possible.

Styles of packets

You can choose between two different foil packet styles, depending on the ingredients you use when you prepare the packet.

The Flat Packet

This type of packet is tighter and keeps the ingredients closer together. It produces less steam and it is perfect for meals you want charred or seared. Note that less steam means less moisture in flat packets, which is why you need to be sure that you have enough ingredients with moisture and not only dry ingredients. Only when you are sure of this should you begin the cooking process. Trust me, just adding some butter is more than enough to make a difference between a juicy steak and the one that is dry and tough.

What you need to do to make a flat packet is take a sheet of aluminum foil and spray it on the inside. Lay the foil on a flat surface and put your ingredients in the middle, layering in accordance with the type and size of the ingredients. Do not spread out your ingredients too much. They should be compact and you will need some free surface around the outside foil edges.

Take two longer foil edges and fold them up to meet in the center. Then make large downward folds toward your ingredients. Bring the packet's short ends in toward the middle and crimp the foil to form a secure, tight packet. When putting the packet on your heat source, make sure to place the folded side up.

The Tent Packet

When you need more steaming and heat circulation, you should opt to use tent packets. Any packet that contains grains or produce will be better cooked in a tent packet. Actually, the only difference between the two styles is that there is more space between the top of the packet and the food, but this allows the food to steam.

Tent packets are made so the top doesn't touch your food. Leave about one to three inches of space above your ingredients. Use a large piece of heavy-duty aluminum foil (remember to spray it), and make sure it is big enough to fit all your ingredients. Allow more foil around the sides because you want enough space for airflow at the top. You also need enough left to make a secure crimp at the top.

Put your ingredients in the middle of the foil. Fold up the long ends of the foils over the food, meeting in the center a couple of inches above the ingredients. Use small folds to crease the foil until you are sure that its top is about three inches distant from the food. Crimp the top tightly. Bring in the sides just close enough to produce a strong seal on each side. When putting the packet over a heat source, place the folded side up.

Keep in Mind That You're Not at Home

We all feel at ease when cooking in our own kitchen, but this is not necessarily true when we are cooking outdoors. Cooking at a campsite is not the same as cooking in your kitchen, so you should always be prepared. You need to modify cooking times in accordance with the situation at that particular moment, and be aware that you can't always predict the time needed for cooking precisely. This is why the best idea is to buy a meat thermometer, which is the most reliable way of checking the temperature of the ingredients you are cooking inside the foil packets. We will discuss this more in the section on the food safety.

At-Home Preparation

The point of foil packet cooking is for everything to be simple at your campsite. If you prepare your food properly at home, you won't have to waste any time on it when you are at the site. There are people who like to prepare their foil packets at home, enabling them just to grill them at the campsite, and there are people who enjoy preparing the packet once they arrive at the site. Either way, here are some tips that will help you.

If you choose to prepare your packets ahead of time

Make sure to select solid fruits and vegetables, as well as other ingredients that hold their structure. Avoid ingredients that might get soggy when combined with juices, oils, and marinades.

Prepare your marinade in a separate container, rather than trying to mix the ingredients in the foil. Marinate the ingredients ahead of time. When marinating the ingredients and placing liquid seasonings into a foil packet, you need to make sure that folds and crimps are strong enough to hold them.

Always keep in mind your safety and think of how you will store foil packets before using them. Any packets that have dairy, fish, or meat should be kept cool. You can add additional protection by putting an assembled foil packet into a food storage bag. Label the bags clearly with the contents. This will enable you to avoid any cross-contamination if a foil packet leaks.

To partially assemble your packets at home

Food storage bags and jars for spices are something you will definitely want to use. You will find that numerous recipes in this book include spices. Don't plan to bring every spice jar you have at home. Instead, prepare a couple of blends of spices in advance and keep them in plastic food bags or jars. Note that it is not recommended for the spices to be stored in plastic bags for a long time, but if you just need to get through the weekend, you can use them without any worry.

Make sure to pre-cut and portion all of the ingredients, and use separate food bags or containers for each one. If you plan on using a lot of chopped onions, you can prepare an entire bag of them.

Another good idea is to prepare sets of ingredients. For example, if you want to prepare a chicken and vegetable foil packet, then you can put sliced chicken in a marinade and spices in one storage bag and pre-cut vegetables in another bag. A neat trick is to label your bags, so you don't have to think what's in every one of them. You can also record which recipes you prepared the particular bag to be used for. Always keep food safety in mind.

To make things simpler, use some quality ingredients that were pre-made. For example, why waste time making a sauce when you can buy a great sauce and save yourself the time and effort. There are also meals where canned ingredients are equally as good as the fresh ones. Also, you won't have to worry because you don't have to pay attention to keeping an appropriate temperature for safety, and they take less time to cook. To make you campsite cooking even easier, use precooked and quick cook items.

Prepare a couple of additional meals, just in case a recipe doesn't go the way it should, or if it should accidentally burn. This can also come in handy if you prolong your stay for another day or extra people show up for dinner!

GRILLING

When camping, most parks and campground provide a fire pit with a grate. Those can be tricky as you don't know how well they have been cleaned and sometimes they look like they have been used since the caveman era! I like to bring my own portable barbecue grill. There are two main advantages in using a portable barbecue.

1. It's easy to set -up and you will be able to start cooking more quickly compared to starting a fire.
2. It's easier to adjust the cooking temperature and you will cook your food more evenly.

Grilling is one of the easiest methods to use to cook food outdoors be it in the backyard or at the campsite. The foundations are the same:

- Prepare your grate in advance by cleaning it thoroughly and oiling it so the food won't stick.
- Pre-heat your grill. If it's a charcoal grill, light it up about 30 minutes before you want to start cooking the food. well in advance to start cooking. For a propane barbecue, about 10 minutes will be enough to reach the desired temperature.
- If you have a temperature indicator, bring it to the temperature required before grilling.
- If the temperature cannot be controlled and becomes too hot, you can use aluminum trays to cook your food on. It will prevent over-cooking and charring your food.
- If you are using the campsite grate, it makes sense to use aluminum trays or at least an aluminum foil sheet on which you cook your food. It can prevent cross-contamination, rust particles mixing in with your food and makes it safer unless you can clean the grate thoroughly.

- Use long tongs and spatula as well as pot holders to protect your hands when manipulating the food being grilled.
- Bring a meat thermometer to make sure your food is cooked to the desired doneness.

Here is a practical chart for barbecue grilling time you can use for all your barbecue cooking for your favorite meats and poultry with some barbecue tips.

Barbecue Grilling Times

BEEF	Size	Grilling Time	Internal Temperature in °F (Fahrenheit)
Steaks	3/4" thick	3 to 4 min/side	Medium rare 145
		4 to 5 min/side	Medium 160
Kabobs	1 inch cubes	3 to 4 min/side	145 to 160
Hamburger patties	1/2" thick	3 min/side	160
Roast, rolled rump (indirect heat)	4 to 6 lbs.	18 to 22 min/lb.	145 to 160
Sirloin tip (indirect heat)	3 1/2 to 4 lbs.	20 to 25 min/lb.	
Ribs, Back	cut in 1 rib portions	10 min/side	160
Tenderloin	Half, 2 to 3 lbs.	10 to 12 min/side	Medium rare 145
	Whole, 4 to 6 lbs.	12 to 15 min/side	Medium 160

PORK	Size	Grilling Time	Internal Temperature in °F (Fahrenheit)

Chops, bone in or boneless	3/4" thick 1 1/2" thick	3 to 4 min/side 7 to 8 min/side	145
Tenderloin	1/2 to 1 1/2 lbs.	15 to 25 min. total	145
Ribs (indirect heat)	2 to 4 lbs.	1 1/2 to 2 hrs.	145
Patties, ground	1/2" thick	4 to 5 min/side	145

HAM	Size	Grilling Time	Internal Temperature in °F (Fahrenheit)
Fully cooked (indirect heat)	any size	8 to 10 min/lb.	140
Cook before eating (indirect heat)	Whole, 10 to 14 lbs. Half, 5 to 7 lbs. Portion, 3 to 4 lbs.	10 to 15 min/lb. 12 to 18 min/lb. 30 to 35 min/lb.	160

LAMB	Size	Grilling Time	Internal Temperature in °F (Fahrenheit)
Chops, shoulder, loin, or rib	1" thick	5 min/side	145 to 160
Steaks, sirloin, or leg	1" thick	5 min/side	145 to 160
Kabobs	1" cubes	4 min/side	145 to 160
Patties, ground	4 oz., 1/2" thick	3 min/side	160
Leg, butterflied	4 to 7 lbs.	40 to 50 min. total	145 to 160
Chops, steaks	1" thick	5 to 7 min/side	145 to 160
Roast, boneless (indirect heat)	2 to 3 lbs.	18 to 20 min/lb.	145 to 160

CHICKEN	Size	Grilling Time	Internal Temperature in °F (Fahrenheit)
Whole (indirect heat), not stuffed	3 to 4 lbs. 5 to 7 lbs. 4 to 8 lbs.	60 to 75 min. 18 to 25 min/lb. 15 to 20 min/lb. 45 to 55 min.	165 to 180 as measured in the thigh
Cornish hens	18 to 24 oz.		
Breast halves, bone in boneless	6 to 8 oz. each 4 oz. each	10 to 15 min/side 7 to 8 min./side –	165 to 170
Other parts: Legs or thighs	4 to 8 oz.	10 to 15 min/side	
Drumsticks	4 oz.	8 to 12 min/side	165 to 180
Wings,	2 to 3 oz.	8 to 12 min/side	

30

TURKEY	Size	Grilling Time	Internal Temperature in °F (Fahrenheit)
Whole turkey (indirect heat)	8 to 12 lbs. 12 to 16 lbs. 16 to 24 lbs.	2 to 3 hrs. 3 to 4 hrs. 4 to 5 hrs.	165 to 180 as measured in the thigh
Breast, bone in boneless	4 to 7 lbs. 2 3/4 to 3 1/2 lbs.	1 to 1 3/4 hrs. 12 to 15 min/side	165 to 170
Thighs, drumsticks (indirect heat) Direct heat (precook 1 hr.)	8 to 16 oz.	1 1/2 to 2 hrs. 8 to 10 min/side	165 to 180
Boneless turkey roll (indirect heat)	2 to 5 lbs. 5 to 10 lbs.	1 1/2 to 2 hrs. 2 to 3 1/2 hrs.	165 to 175

Tips for successful and safe barbecuing:

- To make sure that harmful bacteria, sometime present in uncooked meat and poultry, are destroyed during the cooking process, you must make sure that the internal temperature is high enough for safe consumption. Always use a meat thermometer inserted in the thickest part without touching any bones. Research from the U.S. Department of Agriculture (USDA) states that the color of the meat is not a dependable indicator meat or poultry has reached a temperature high enough to destroy harmful bacteria that may be present.

- Follow this chart for approximate cooking times, Outdoor grills can vary in heat.

- Use barbecue sauce during the last 15 to 30 minutes of grilling to prevent excess browning or burning resulting from the sugars of the sauce.

31

- USDA recommends cooking pork, beef, veal, lamb chops, ribs and steaks until it reaches a minimum internal temperature of 145ºF and then let rest at least 3 minutes before slicing or consuming.

- Although it is safe to eat poultry with an internal temperature of 165°F, the flavors and the texture are best when the internal temperature reaches 170°F to 180°F

Source: Food Safety and Inspection Service, USDA

CAST IRON DUTCH OVEN

Choosing Your Cast Iron Dutch Oven

When it comes to purchasing a Dutch oven, you will find that you have many options to choose from. The choices may seem overwhelming. No matter what brands and price points you care to consider, there are some basic features to pay attention to when it comes to choosing your Dutch oven.

The first is size. A good size for a Dutch oven to take camping is 12-16 inches. Anything smaller than that may not allow you enough space to cook entire meals for multiple people. However, if you are a solo or couples-only camper, you may be able to get away with a smaller model. A 12-inch Dutch oven offers you enough room to prepare medium-sized meals. It fits in nicely at most campsite heat sources and is not so large and heavy that it becomes overly cumbersome to transport.

The next feature you want to look at when choosing a Dutch oven is the type of lid you prefer. Many manufacturers of Dutch ovens assume that they will be used primarily in the home and therefore can be missing some of the necessary features that you may need for cooking at your campsite. When choosing your Dutch oven, pick one that is not only tight fitting, but also has a bit of a concave curve to it, as well as at least a small rim around the edge. This will provide a stable surface for placing hot coals on top of your oven. Also, make sure that the lid has a solid handle that is large enough to be lifted with a lid lifter device.

Finally, choose a Dutch oven with good legs. It should have three evenly spaced legs that raise the oven at least an inch off of the ground. Good legs provide a stable cooking surface that allows plenty of room for hot coals to be placed underneath.

Cast Iron Dutch Oven How-To

Cooking with cast iron requires a few extra steps for maintenance, but there's no doubt that the results are worth it! Here are a few pieces of advice concerning care, upkeep, and use of your cast iron Dutch oven.

Seasoning your cast iron cookware

The first thing you need to know about cast iron care is seasoning. Seasoning is the process of applying oil to your cast iron, initially to remove contaminants, and then to prevent rust, corrosion, and baked-on food particles from degrading your cookware. The only time you ever need to use dish detergent on your cast iron is the first time you season it. To do that, scrub the inside and the outside of the oven with a hot, soapy mixture. Dry it thoroughly with a cloth, and then place it on a very hot heat source to finish drying the surface. Once it is completely dry, rub oil or fat (not butter) into the surface, both inside and out. Once the oven has been coated, take another cloth and continue to rub and polish the oven until it appears that there is no oily residue left. Place the oven back on the heat source for about an hour, flipping it over halfway through. Remove from the heat and let cool before handling. Depending on the oven, you may want to repeat this process several times before using it for the first time; repeated seasonings help to condition the cast iron and provide an attractive surface sheen. Season the oven again periodically throughout its life as you see fit.

Cleaning

Cleaning cast iron is a little different from cleaning other cookware. After using your Dutch oven, remove as much food from it as you can. While it's still warm, add about an inch or more of water and let it sit with the lid on. After 15–20 minutes, remove the lid and scrape off any remaining food bits. Discard the dirty water and repeat the process with clean water until the oven is free of food residue. Dry the inside thoroughly with a cloth and place the oven back on the warm coals to help drive off the remaining moisture. Once the oven is dry and cool, apply a very light layer of vegetable oil to the surface inside and out.

Cooking with a Cast Iron Dutch Oven at the Campsite

When using a cast iron Dutch oven at your campsite, you will usually be applying heat to both the top and the bottom by means of charcoal briquettes. The recipes in this book assume a temperature of approximately 350°F. In order to achieve this, you will use briquettes in numbers that are proportional to the size of your oven. A general rule is to use at least twice as many briquettes as the diameter of your oven. For example, if you have a 12-inch oven, you will use 24 pieces of charcoal. A 16-inch oven would require approximately 32. This, however, is a very generalized rule that should only serve as a guideline and will also depends on the temperature you want to cook your food as you will see in the table below. Always use a thermometer when you are learning to gauge the temperature of your oven, especially if you are using wood rather than coals.

Here is a table that gives you a general idea of the number of hot coals you will need according to the size of your cast iron Dutch oven and the desired cooking temperature.

Dutch Oven Temperature Chart
Number of Charcoal Briquettes Required

Temp.→ Oven Size ↓	325°F 163°C	350°F 177°C	375°F 191°C	400°F 204°C	425°F 218°C	450°F 232°C
8 inches	Top: 10 Bottom: 5 Total: 15	Top: 11 Bottom: 5 Total: 16	Top: 11 Bottom: 6 Total: 17	Top: 12 Bottom: 6 Total: 18	Top: 13 Bottom: 6 Total: 19	Top: 14 Bottom: 6 Total: 20
10 inches	Top: 13 Bottom: 6 Total: 19	Top: 14 Bottom: 7 Total: 21	Top: 16 Bottom: 7 Total: 23	Top: 17 Bottom: 8 Total: 25	Top: 18 Bottom: 9 Total: 27	Top: 19 Bottom: 10 Total: 29
12 inches	Top: 16 Bottom: 7 Total: 23	Top: 17 Bottom: 8 Total: 25	Top: 18 Bottom: 9 Total: 27	Top: 19 Bottom: 10 Total: 29	Top: 21 Bottom: 10 Total: 31	Top: 22 Bottom: 11 Total: 33
14 inches	Top: 20 Bottom: 10 Total: 30	Top: 21 Bottom: 11 Total: 32	Top: 22 Bottom: 12 Total: 34	Top: 24 Bottom: 12 Total: 36	Top: 25 Bottom: 13 Total: 38	Top: 26 Bottom: 14 Total: 40
16 inches	Top: 25 Bottom: 12 Total: 37	Top: 26 Bottom: 13 Total: 39	Top: 27 Bottom: 14 Total: 41	Top: 28 Bottom: 15 Total: 43	Top: 29 Bottom: 16 Total: 45	Top: 30 Bottom: 17 Total: 47

By no mean is this chart an exact science! But it gives a good indication of the cooking temperature according to the size of cast iron Dutch oven you are using and the number of coals you will

35

approximately need. Remember to replenish as the coals cool down, especially if you are preparing a dish that requires several hours of cooking.

With wind, more oxygen is added to the cooking environment, which causes coal to emit more heat at once, shortening its burning time. Wind can also blow away the heat, so it'd be wise to block the wind around the Dutch oven when it's windy. This can be done with aluminum foil, rocks, logs, there are even stove windscreens and camping tables tailored for this purpose, among others.

The ground is another factor to keep in mind. Moist cold ground takes heat away and can even extinguish the charcoal. Setting up a dry surface below the charcoal to keep it unaffected by the ground is the way to go.

The colder the air is, it's more difficult to heat the Dutch oven. It's the same with higher elevation (due to air density) and humidity. More sunlight means more to be absorbed and turned into heat, especially when the cast iron Dutch oven is black due to the color's properties. When it's really warm, the sunlight can even be too much, so covering it with a camping canopy is a good idea, and it can also serve from guarding the charcoal against the rain. When it's too humid to light the charcoal briquettes, you may need to use a chimney starter.

While the above table is for the cast iron Dutch oven, both it and the aluminum version have their advantages and disadvantages. Aluminum Dutch ovens are a third of the weight of the cast iron ones. They also do not rust, are easy to clean and heat up more quickly, requiring about ¾ as much coal than their cast iron counterparts. Cast iron Dutch ovens, on the other side, retain heat longer and distribute it more evenly, which is often desired for preparing food.

Placement of the coals on the bottom and/or lid

Where you place the coals, and in what numbers, also depends on the method of cooking. Different quantities and configurations can help distribute the heat properly or concentrate it to a critical area. For sautéing, boiling, frying, or open lid cooking, you will place all of the coals underneath the oven. For methods of cooking that require both a top and bottom heat source, distribute the coals between the bottom and the top of the lid. Depending on the proportion of heat that you need from each heat source, you can divide them up with half on top and half on the bottom, or ¾ on the bottom and ¼ on top. Give yourself a little time to practice adjusting the heat on your Dutch oven before creating more involved meals. Here is a general guideline depending on the cooking method you are using.

1. **For roasting**, coal in the Dutch oven should be split evenly between top and bottom.
2. **For baking**, ¾ should be on top and ¼ on the bottom.
3. **For simmering and stewing**, 4/5 should be on top, and 1/5 on the bottom.
4. **For frying and boiling**, all coals should be on the bottom part.

To check the temperature of the food, use an instant-read meat thermometer easily available online and in kitchen supply stores. If you happen to forget a thermometer or just don't want to use one, you can also rely on your sense of smell. Generally speaking, if the food doesn't emit anything that you can smell, it is not done, and if it smells burnt, it is burning or starting to, time to take it off the heat and hope it's not all burned. If it smells really good and profusely, it's probably done or nearly so.

Cooking with your Dutch oven outside is a little different from using it indoors, and it requires a few pieces of additional equipment. First of all, you definitely want a good, reliable lid lifting device. Cast iron can get very hot, especially if you have hot coals placed on the lid. To protect yourself from burns, use a heat protective glove or mitt along with a lid lifting device to remove the lid. A lid stand is also a good idea. This will provide a heat-proof resting place for your lid so you won't have to set it down on the dirty ground. You may also find a long pair of tongs helpful for moving hot coal briquettes. If you spend a great deal of time cooking in the great outdoors, at some point you may wish to invest in either a tripod or a Dutch oven cooking table. These devices are a little more cumbersome than the Dutch oven alone, but they provide a more stable, safer cooking environment.

CAMPFIRE COOKING

This cookbook includes recipes for both grilling on a wire grate/grill as well as cooking on a stick or on a spit over an open fire. You will need skewers for grilling on a wire rack or grill. Alternatively, you will need to find sticks out in the wild for cooking over the open fire or bring some with you.

Choosing Sticks for Spit Roasting

When looking for your campfire stick, make sure it is long enough for you to hold over a fire without your hand having to be too close to the fire.

Also, make sure the stick is nice and sturdy. The last thing you want is your tasty kebob landing in the fire a minute before it should have been landing in your mouth.

First, you need to figure out how wide your fire pit is so that you can find a stick that will fit across and hold.

Secondly you want to find a stick that has branches halfway down the center so that you can more easily secure your food.

You also need two additional, y-shaped sticks to balance your spit stick on. Make sure your sticks are high enough that the food won't burn in the fire.

HEALTHY CAMPING MENUS AND RECIPES

2-DAY HEALTHY CAMPING MENUS

Day One

Breakfast: Healthy Omelet
Lunch: Southwestern Pasta
Supper: Garlic Lemon Chicken Rice Skillet
Dessert: Oatmeal Cranberry Baked Apples

Day Two

Breakfast: Bistro Panini
Lunch: Tomato Chickpea Soup
Supper: Mexican-inspired Chicken and Veggies Foil Packet
Dessert: Campfire Cones

SHOPPING LIST

Fats
Butter, 6 tablespoons
Olive oil, 3 tablespoons

Meats and other proteins
Almond butter, 1 tablespoon
Chicken breast, 3 pounds
Chopped pecans, ¼ cup
Turkey bacon, 12 slices

Vegetables and fruits
Apples: 5
Banana, 1
Beans, green, fresh, 2 cups
Cranberries, dried, 2 tablespoons
Garlic, 6 cloves
Lemon, 1
Mushrooms, 1 cup, sliced
Onion, red, 2
Onion, yellow, 2
Pepper, green 2
Pepper, red sweet, 1
Pepper, yellow sweet, 1
Spinach, baby, 2 cups
Strawberries, halved, 1 cup
Tomatoes, cherry, 1 cup

Dairies
Brie (or another soft cheese of your choice), 4 ounces
Eggs, 8

Grains
Basmati rice, 1 ½ cups, dry
Bread, whole grain, 8 thick slices
Pasta, whole wheat, 8 ounces dry (4 cups cooked)
Rolled oats, 3 tablespoons
Waffle cones, 4

Cans

Black beans, 1 (8-ounce) can
Chicken broth, 2 (8-ounce) cans
Chickpeas, 1 (15-ounce) can
Corn, 1 can
Crushed tomatoes, 1 (28-ounce) can
Tomato paste, 2 tablespoons
Tomatoes with chilies, diced, 1 (8-ounce)

Seasonings and toppings

Brown sugar, 2 tablespoons
Chocolate chips, ½ cup
Cinnamon
Hot sauce
Jam, 4 tablespoons
Marshmallows, mini, 1 cup
Pepper
Salt
Taco seasoning, lower sodium, 4 tablespoons

DAY ONE RECIPES

Breakfast: Healthy Omelet

You'll love this very simple, nutritious and warm egg omelet recipe that can be prepared easily while camping.

Serves 4

Ingredients
1 tablespoon butter
12 slices turkey bacon, chopped
1 cup mushrooms, sliced
8 eggs, beaten
1 cup cherry tomatoes, halved
1 cup baby spinach, chopped

Directions
1. Place a frying pan on a rack over hot coals, and melt the butter in it.
2. Add the turkey bacon and cook for 5 minutes, or until crisp. Set 8 slices aside for another recipe, and chop the remaining 4 for the omelet.
3. Add the mushrooms and stir for 5 minutes.
4. Pour the eggs into the pan and add the tomatoes and spinach.
5. When the eggs begin to set, gently lift the edge of the omelet and allow the liquid egg to flow under the cooked layer. Cover the pan and let it cook over low heat until the omelet is set. Do not stir.

Lunch: Southwestern Pasta

This colorful vegetarian pasta dish is loaded with fiber and flavor.

Serves 4

Ingredients
8 ounces whole wheat pasta (4 cups cooked)
1 teaspoon extra virgin olive oil
1 small red onion, chopped
1 small green bell pepper, cut into thin strips
2 tablespoons lower-sodium taco seasoning
1 (8-ounce) can tomatoes and chilies
1 (12-ounce) can corn
2 cups water
1 (8-ounce) can black beans, drained and rinsed

Directions
1. Prepare the pasta by boiling it in water until al dente.
2. Heat the oil in a large pot over medium heat.
3. Add the onion, bell pepper, and seasoning. Sauté until fragrant (about 1 minute).
4. Stir in the canned tomatoes and corn. Cook a bit until bubbly.
5. Stir in the water and bring the pot to a simmer. Let it cook, stirring frequently, until reduced and of desired consistency (about 10–15 minutes).
6. Add the cooked pasta and mix. Cook until heated through.
7. Add the black beans and remove the pot from the heat.
8. Let it sit until the beans are heated through.

Supper: Garlic Lemon Chicken Rice Skillet

This one-pot meal is aromatic and easy to make.

Serves 4

Ingredients
1 ½ pounds chicken, sliced into strips
1 tablespoon butter
1 yellow onion, diced
1 cup Basmati rice
2 cups chicken broth
4 cloves garlic, minced
Salt and pepper to taste
1 lemon, sliced
2 cups fresh green beans

Directions
1. Prepare the Dutch oven over 18 coals.
2. Once the oven is hot, add the butter, chicken, and onion. Toss while cooking for 5 minutes.
3. Add the rice, chicken broth, and garlic. Cook for 5–7 minutes.
4. Season with salt and pepper. Top with sliced lemons and green beans and cover the Dutch oven.
5. Cook for 25 minutes, or until the chicken is cooked through and the rice is tender.

Dessert: Oatmeal Cranberry Baked Apples

Your campers will love this healthy baked dessert.

Serves 4

Ingredients
4 medium apples
2 tablespoons butter
1 tablespoon almond butter
2 tablespoons dried cranberries, chopped
3 tablespoons rolled oats
½ teaspoon cinnamon
2 tablespoons brown sugar
¼ cup chopped pecans

Directions
1. Lay out four pieces of foil and lightly coat each with butter or coconut oil.
2. Wash and core the apples (don't slice or chop them), being careful not to pierce the bottom.
3. In a small bowl, combine the butter, almond butter, cranberries, rolled oats, cinnamon, brown sugar, and pecans. Mix well.
4. Divide the mixture among the apples, pressing it down into the cavity.
5. Wrap the apples in the foil and place them near the fire or directly on the grill. Cook for about 20 minutes, until softened.

DAY TWO RECIPES

Breakfast: Bistro Panini

Try this unique version of a gourmet breakfast sandwich, balancing the savory bacon and cheese with the sweet of the jam.

Serves 4

Ingredients
8 slices turkey bacon
2 tablespoons butter
4 ounces of soft cheese (like brie), sliced
8 thick slices whole grain bread
4 tablespoons of your favorite jam (suggested: raspberry, fig, plum)

* For vegetarians, there are bacon substitutes or try thin slices of mushroom.

Directions
1. Preheat a cast iron skillet over medium heat.
2. Butter the outsides of the bread. Spread the jam on one side, and then place the cheese on top. Add the bacon and put the sandwich together.
3. Place the sandwich, butter side down, on the preheated pan. With your spatula, press down on the sandwich. Allow the bread to toast on one side, then flip the sandwich over. Cook for 1–2 minutes per side, until it's golden brown and the cheese has melted.

Lunch: Tomato Chickpea Soup

This is not your old-fashioned tomato soup! Adjust the heat to your liking in this nutritious vegan meal.

Serves 4

Ingredients
2 tablespoons olive oil
1 medium yellow onion, diced
2 cloves garlic, minced
1 cup spinach, chopped
1 (28-ounce) can crushed tomatoes
2 cups water
½ cup basmati rice, rinsed
2 tablespoons tomato paste
1 (15-ounce) can chickpeas, drained and rinsed
Salt, pepper, and hot sauce to taste

Directions
1. In your Dutch oven over 18 coals, warm the oil and sauté the onion for 3–5 minutes. Stir in the garlic and cook until fragrant.
2. Add the spinach and stir a minute or two, until it begins to wilt.
3. Add the tomatoes, water, and rice. Bring the mixture to a boil and let it simmer for 15–20 minutes.
4. Add the tomato paste, chickpeas, salt, pepper, and hot sauce. Cook to heat through, and serve.

Supper: Mexican-inspired Chicken and Veggies Foil Packet

Wrapped in aluminum foil and cooked over the grill, this spicy Mexican-inspired dish is packed with yummy chicken and vegetables, making it as delicious as it is hearty.

Serves 4

Ingredients
1 ½ pounds chicken breasts, boneless and skinless, cut into strips
2 tablespoons lower-sodium taco seasoning
1 red bell pepper, cut into strips
1 green bell pepper, cut into strips
1 yellow bell pepper, cut into strips
1 red onion, cut into strips

Directions
1. In a bowl, toss the chicken strips with the taco seasoning.
2. Lay 4 large sheets of heavy-duty foil on a flat surface. Pour even amounts of prepared ingredients onto the center of each sheet. For each sheet, fold all 4 edges and roll at the middle to seal tightly.
3. Place foil packets on the grill over indirect heat. Cook for about 20–25 minutes until the chicken is cooked through.

Dessert: Campfire Cones

These easy and customizable fruit cups are surprisingly easy – you'll wonder why you never thought of this!

Serves 4

Ingredients
4 waffle cones
1 cup strawberries, chopped
1 apple, diced
1 banana, chopped
½ cup chocolate chips
1 cup mini marshmallows

Directions
1. Combine the fillings and spoon them into the waffle cones
2. Wrap each cone in a piece of foil and place them near the fire. Rotate them often.
3. Cook for 5–7 minutes.

3-DAY HEALTHY CAMPING MENU

Day One
Breakfast: Backcountry Oatmeal Breakfast
Lunch: Tuna Burgers
Supper: Almond Chicken
Dessert: Berry Grunt

Day Two
Breakfast: Egg White Omelet
Lunch: BBQ Chicken Rainbow Pasta Salad
Supper: Dutch Oven Pot Roast
Dessert: Pineapple Berry Pack

Day Three
Breakfast: Banana Paleo Pancakes
Lunch: Light Philly Cheese Wraps
Supper: Curried Chickpea Buddha Bowls
Dessert: Healthy Coconut Coffee Cake

SHOPPING LIST

<u>Fats</u>
Butter, ½ cup
Coconut oil, ¾ cup plus 1 tablespoon

Olive oil, 3 tablespoons

Meats and other proteins
Almond butter, ½ cup
Almonds, slivered, 1 ½ cups
Chicken breasts, 5-ounce, 6
Coconut, shredded, ⅓ cup
Eggs, whites only, 8
Eggs, whole, 10
Nuts, mixed, unsalted, chopped, ½ cup
Sirloin tip roast, 2 ½ pounds
Tuna, 5-ounce cans, 2

Vegetables and fruits
Bananas, 6
Berries, fresh, mixed, 7 cups
Cabbage, purple, shredded, 1 cup
Carrots, 3
Cherry tomatoes, halved, ½ cup
Cucumber, 1
Green bell pepper, 1
Lemon, 1
Onions, sweet, 3
Pineapple, fresh, 1
Raisins (or dried apples) ½ cup
Spinach, chopped, ½ cup
Sweet potato, 2
Tomato, 3
White potato, large, 1
Yellow bell pepper, 2

Dairies
Cheddar cheese, shredded, 1 cup
Milk, 1%, ½ cup plus 2 tablespoons
Parmesan, grated, 2 tablespoons

Powdered milk, non-fat, ½ cup
Provolone cheese, 4 ounces

Grains
Almond flour, ½ cup
Brown rice, dry, 2 cups
Coconut flour, ⅓ cup
Flour, all-purpose, 2 tablespoons
Penne, whole wheat, dry, 2 cups
Quick-cooking or instant oats, 1 ½ cups
Sandwich buns, whole wheat, 4
Tortillas, whole wheat, 10-inch, 4

Cans
Beef stock, 2 cups
Chickpeas, 15-ounce, 1
Coconut milk, ½ cup
Corn, 12-ounce, 1
Diced tomatoes, 15-ounce, 1

Seasonings, toppings, others
*Cayenne pepper, pinch
*Hummus, ½ cup
*Lemon juice, 1 tablespoon
*Maple syrup, 1 tablespoon
Baking powder, 2 teaspoons
Baking soda, 1 ¼ teaspoons
Chili powder, ½ teaspoon
Cinnamon, 2 tablespoons
Coffee, ½ cup
Curry powder, 1 teaspoon
Garlic powder, ½ teaspoon
Honey, ½ cup
Mayonnaise, light, ⅓ cup
Pepper

Red wine, ¼ cup
Rosemary, dried, 1 teaspoon
Salt
Sugar, brown, 5 tablespoons
Sugar, white, 6 tablespoons
Thyme, dried, 2 teaspoons

*These items can be combined at home for the Buddha bowl on day three.

DAY ONE RECIPES

Breakfast: Backcountry Oatmeal Breakfast

This is a big upgrade from your regular instant oatmeal, but it's just as easy as the packaged kind.

Serves 4

Ingredients
1 ½ cups quick-cooking or instant oats
½ cup powdered milk (non-fat)
½ cup raisins or dried apple bits
½ cup unsalted mixed nuts, chopped
3 tablespoons brown sugar
1 teaspoon cinnamon
Pinch salt
4 cups boiling water

Directions
1. Prepare in advance, if desired. Combine all the ingredients EXCEPT the boiling water in a resealable bag, shaking to mix. Set it aside until ready for use.
2. To serve, place the mixture in a bowl and add boiling water. Let sit for 2 minutes. Mix and serve.

Lunch: Tuna Burgers

This classic is so easy to make at the campsite.

Serves 4

Ingredients
2 (5-ounce) cans tuna
½ sweet onion, chopped
⅓ cup light mayonnaise
1 teaspoon black pepper
4 whole wheat sandwich buns
½ cup shredded cheddar cheese

Directions
1. Prepare 4 sheets of foil large enough to hold the buns.
2. Drain the tuna and place it in a bowl. Break it apart with a fork.
3. Add the onion, mayonnaise, and black pepper.
4. Divide the mixture among the buns, and top with a portion of the cheese.
5. Fold the foil to make flat packets.
6. Grill for approximately 10 minutes.

Supper: Almond Chicken

These easy and tasty foil packets are easy to prepare. They're very versatile, but today we're going with almonds, rosemary, and corn.

Serves 4

Ingredients
1 tablespoon coconut oil
6 (5-ounce) boneless skinless chicken breasts*
Salt and pepper to taste
½ cup slivered almonds
1 teaspoon rosemary
2 cups dry brown rice**
1 (12-ounce) can corn
½ cucumber, sliced

* 2 are for lunch the next day
** Half this rice is for a later recipe

Directions
1. Lay out 6 pieces of foil and lightly coat them with coconut oil.
2. Arrange a chicken breast on each piece of foil. Season them with salt and pepper.
3. Fold TWO of the packets closed and set them aside.
4. For the remaining FOUR packets, sprinkle on the almonds and rosemary. Close the packets and place them on a grill over medium heat. Cook for 30–40 minutes, until the internal temperature reaches 165°F.
5. Meanwhile, boil two cups of water and cook the rice. Chill half the rice for supper on day two.
6. Heat the corn.
7. Wash and slice the cucumber.
8. Chill the two unseasoned chicken breasts and serve the remaining four with rice, corn, and cucumber.

Dessert: Berry Grunt

Break out your cast iron skillet and whip up this tart and tasty dessert in just over half an hour. Your campers will appreciate it!

Serves 4

Ingredients
6 cups fresh mixed berries (blueberries, raspberries, and blackberries)
¼ cup sugar
2 tablespoons water

For the topping:
1 cup all-purpose flour
2 tablespoons sugar
1 teaspoon baking powder
½ teaspoon baking soda
½ cup plus 2 tablespoons milk
2 tablespoons butter, melted

Directions
1. In a skillet over medium heat, combine the berries, sugar, and water. Cook until they begin to thicken, about 10–15 minutes.
2. In a separate bowl, combine the flour, baking powder, sugar, and baking soda. (This step can be done at home, and brought to the campsite in a resealable bag.)
3. Mix in the milk and butter.
4. When the berries have thickened, spoon the topping on in small dollops.
5. Cover the skillet with foil, and cook for about 20 minutes, until the dumplings are cooked through.

DAY TWO RECIPES

Breakfast: Egg White Omelet

These healthy omelets dish out a serving of vegetables and 10 grams of protein! Serve with a slice of whole grain toast if you like, or a piece of fruit.

Serves 4

Ingredients
8 large egg whites
½ teaspoon salt
¼ teaspoon freshly ground black pepper
½ cup firm cherry tomatoes, halved
½ cup spinach, chopped
1 tablespoon olive oil
2 tablespoons grated Parmesan cheese

Directions
1. Place a skillet over medium heat.
2. Combine two of the egg whites in a mixing bowl and whisk until frothy. Stir in a quarter of the salt and pepper, cherry tomatoes, and spinach.
3. Heat a quarter of the oil in the pan, and pour in the egg mixture. Be very mindful of the heat, and lift the skillet off the coals or stove if the egg is browning too quickly.
4. As the egg sets, lift the edge of the omelet with the spatula, and allow the uncooked egg to go under the cooked portion. When it's nearly set, flip it over.
5. Sprinkle the top with half a tablespoon of the Parmesan. Fold the omelet in half, and cook until golden and cooked through.

Supper: Dutch Oven Pot Roast

Hungry after a long day outdoors? This hearty pot roast is guaranteed to satisfy!

Serves 4

Ingredients
1 boneless sirloin tip roast, approximately 2 ½ pounds, well trimmed
2 tablespoons butter
1 large white potato, cubed
1 sweet potato, peeled and cubed
1 sweet yellow onion, sliced
3 carrots, scrubbed and chopped
2 cups beef stock
1 (15-ounce) can diced tomatoes
¼ cup red wine
2 teaspoons dried thyme
Salt and pepper to taste
2 tablespoons flour
½ cup water

Directions
1. Prepare your Dutch oven by heating the coals and placing the oven over three-quarters of them and adding the remaining quarter on top of the lid.
2. Once the oven is hot, melt the butter. Add the roast and it sear evenly on each for approximately 2 minutes per side.
3. Surround the roast with the potatoes, onion, and carrots.
4. In a separate bowl, combine the beef stock, tomatoes, red wine, bay leaf, thyme, salt, and pepper. Mix well.
5. Pour the mixture over the meat and vegetables.
6. Cover and cook on low for 1–2 hours, turning the roast occasionally, until the meat is tender.

7. Remove the roast from the broth and set it on a platter. Cover it with foil and let it rest while you prepare the gravy.
8. Skim any fat from the broth.
9. Combine the flour with the water and shake or mix vigorously to combine. Stir the mixture into the pot and stir until thickened.
10. Set aside about 10 ounces of the cooked roast for tomorrow's lunch.

Dessert: Pineapple Berry Pack

Pineapple is the chef's kiss of grilled fruit. You won't believe how delicious this simple dessert is!
Serves 4

Ingredients
1 fresh pineapple, peeled and cut in chunks
2 tablespoons brown sugar
2 tablespoons butter
1 cup fresh mixed berries

Directions
1. Prepare 4 sheets of sturdy foil and arrange a portion of the pineapple on each.
2. Sprinkle each with half a tablespoon of brown sugar and dot with half a tablespoon of butter.
3. Fold up the foil and seal it tightly.
4. Place the packets over medium heat and cook for about 10 minutes, turning and rotating them from time to time.
5. Top with fresh berries, and serve.

DAY THREE RECIPES

Breakfast: Banana Paleo Pancakes

With just a few ingredients, you can set your campers up for a happy, busy morning outdoors.

Serves 6

Ingredients
2 tablespoons coconut oil
6 ripe bananas
6 eggs
½ cup almond butter
2 teaspoons cinnamon
½ teaspoon salt

Directions.
1. Place a cast iron skillet over medium heat.
2. Mash the bananas very well, and beat in the eggs until smooth.
3. Stir in the almond butter, cinnamon, and salt.
4. Melt a little of the coconut oil in the skillet and spoon in some batter. Keep the pancakes small so they'll be easy to flip.
5. Cook for 2–3 minutes on each side.
6. Repeat until all the pancakes are cooked

Lunch: Light Philly Cheese Wraps

The flavor you love, the protein you need – without a load of excess fat and calories.

Serves 4

Ingredients

1 tablespoon olive oil

1 sweet onion, sliced

1 green pepper, sliced

10 ounces leftover roast beef, thinly sliced (deli can be used but it's higher in salt and preservatives)

4 (10-inch) whole wheat tortillas

2 tablespoons butter

½ teaspoon garlic powder

4 ounces provolone cheese, sliced

Directions

1. In a skillet over medium heat, warm the oil.
2. Sauté the onion and green pepper until soft. (If you are doing this step at home, let them cool. Transfer them to a resealable bag and refrigerate them.)
3. At the campsite, set out a 4 pieces of aluminum foil and coat them with cooking spray.
4. Combine the butter with the garlic powder, and spread it on the tortillas.
5. Arrange the meat slices on the bread, and top with the vegetable mixture and cheese.
6. Roll up the wraps and wrap them in the foil. Cook over indirect heat for about 10 minutes, turning from time to time, until the bread is warm and the cheese is melted.

Supper: Curried Chickpea Buddha Bowls

The secret to a good Buddha bowl is to combine a variety of colors and textures.

Serves 4

Ingredients
2 tablespoons coconut oil, divided
1 sweet potato, washed and cut in ½-inch cubes
1 teaspoon curry powder
½ teaspoon chili powder
1 can chickpeas
2 cups cooked brown rice (from supper on day one)
1 cup purple cabbage, shredded
1 tomato, diced
1 small yellow pepper, diced

For the sauce
½ cup hummus
1 tablespoon lemon juice
1 tablespoon maple syrup
Pinch cayenne pepper

Directions
1. Prepare the dressing by combining the ingredients. This can be done at home if you like, and the sauce kept in a tightly lidded container.
2. In a skillet over medium heat, warm half the oil and cook the sweet potato. When it is nicely browned, remove it to a covered bowl and keep it warm.
3. Add the remaining oil to the pan, together with the curry powder, chili powder, and red pepper flakes. Cook, stirring, for one minute, to temper the spices.

4. Add the chickpeas and mix well. Cook 3–5 minutes, or until the chickpeas are browned and hot. Remove them from the pan and keep them warm.
5. Tip the leftover rice into the hot skillet and cook to warm it through, 3–5 minutes.
6. Set out four serving bowls and among them, divide the rice, chickpeas, and sweet potato. Add a portion of the cabbage, tomato, and yellow pepper.
7. Top with a drizzle of sauce, and serve.

Dessert: Healthy Coconut Coffee Cake

There is a little mixing involved, but this coffee cake is the perfect finale to your camping trip.

Serves 4

Ingredients
½ cup almond flour
⅓ cup coconut flour
⅓ cup unsweetened shredded coconut
½ cup coconut oil, melted
½ cup coconut milk
½ cup coffee
⅓ cup honey
4 eggs, lightly beaten
1 teaspoon baking soda
1 teaspoon baking powder
½ teaspoon cinnamon
1 pinch salt

For the topping:

2 tablespoons coconut oil

1 cup slivered almonds

3 tablespoons honey

1 teaspoon cinnamon

1 pinch salt

Directions

1. Place a Dutch oven over 18 briquettes, covered, to warm up.
2. In a mixing bowl, combine the cake ingredients and mix just to moisten. Spread the batter in a lightly greased cake pan that fits inside your Dutch oven.
3. Place a trivet or a few stones in the bottom of the Dutch oven, and put in the cake pan. Cover the pot and arrange the briquettes so there are 12 on top and 8 underneath. Try to maintain a temperature of 350°F.
4. Bake for about 20 minutes and then check the progress. You might need up to 30 minutes of baking time.
5. Meanwhile, in a saucepan, prepare the topping. Melt the coconut oil and add the almonds. Cooking over medium heat, brown the almonds. Be careful not to let them burn.
6. Stir in the honey, cinnamon, and salt. Remove the saucepan from the heat and let it sit, stirring occasionally.
7. When the cake is finished spoon the topping over it, pressing gently with the back of the spoon.

5-DAY HEALTHY CAMPING MENU

Day One
Breakfast: Greek Yogurt Parfaits
Lunch: Black Bean Wraps
Supper: Dutch Oven Roast Chicken
Dessert: Foil Apple Crisp

Day Two
Breakfast: Blueberry Chia Pudding
Lunch: Chicken Salad Lettuce Wraps
Supper: Shrimp and Wild Rice
Dessert: No Bake Chocolate Oat Bars

Day Three
Breakfast: Turkey Bacon and Spinach Frittata
Lunch: Chicken Corn Chowder
Supper: Turkey and Chickpea Burgers
Dessert: Lemon Blueberry Biscuits

Day Four
Breakfast: Breakfast BLT Sandwiches
Lunch: Bean Salad
Supper: Rosemary and Lime Steak
Dessert: Watermelon Pizza

Day Five
Quinoa Peach Breakfast
Lunch: Steak Quesadillas
Supper: Pineapple Turkey Skewers
Dessert: Banana Bread

SHOPPING LIST

Fats
Butter, 1 ½ cups
Coconut oil, ½ cup
Olive oil, ½ cup

Meats and other proteins
Coconut, shredded unsweetened, ¾ cup
Chicken, whole, 5 pounds
Eggs, 15
Almond butter, ¾ cup
Shrimp, large or jumbo, 1 pound
Sirloin steaks, 5-ounce, 6
Turkey bacon, 1 pound
Turkey, ground, 2 pounds

Vegetables and fruits
Apples, 5
Avocado, 1
Bananas, 6
Bibb lettuce (or Romaine), 12 leaves
Blueberries, fresh, 2 ½ cups
Carrots, baby, 2 ½ cups
Celery, 4 stalks
Garlic, 2 cloves
Peaches, 2
Pepper, green, 2
Pepper, orange, 1
Kiwis, 2
Lemon, 3

Lime, 1
Mushrooms, 1 cup
Onion, yellow or sweet, 5
Onion, red, 4
Potatoes, white, 10
Snow peas, 2 ½ cups
Spinach, baby, 10 cups
Strawberries, 2 ½ cups
Tomato, 3
Watermelon, 1 small

Dairies
Almond milk (or alternative), 1 quart
Feta cheese, 12 ounces
Greek yogurt, plain, 2%, 2 quarts plus 2 cups
Milk, 1%, 4 ½ cups

Grains
Chia seeds, 1 cup
Flour, white, 3 cups
Flour, whole wheat, 1 cup
Flour tortillas, whole wheat, 10-inch, 8
Hamburger buns, whole wheat, 8
Oats, rolled, 3 ⅓ cups
Quinoa, dry, 2 cups
Rice, long grain and wild blend, 2 cups

Cans
Black beans, 14-ounce, 2 cans
Chickpeas, 14-ounce, 2 cans
Corn, 14-ounce, 3 cans
Pineapple, 14-ounce, 1 can

Seasonings, toppings, others

Baking powder, 2 teaspoons

Baking soda, 2 teaspoons

Brown sugar, 1 ½ cups

Cinnamon, 2 teaspoons

Garlic powder, 3 teaspoons

Italian seasoning, 1 ½ teaspoons

Maple syrup, 1 cup plus 4 teaspoons

Pepper, black

Pickles, for turkey burgers, optional

Rosemary sprigs, fresh, 4

Salsa, 1 cup

Salt

Sugar, icing, 1 cup

Sugar, white, ¾ cup

Vinegar, balsamic, 3 tablespoons

DAY ONE RECIPES

Breakfast: Greek Yogurt Parfaits

Everyone loves the colorful layers of a parfait. With Greek yogurt and crunchy, fresh granola, this version will keep you going until lunchtime.

Serves 4

Ingredients
For the granola:
2 tablespoons coconut oil
2 cups rolled oats
¼ cup brown sugar
1 teaspoon cinnamon

4 cups 2% plain Greek yogurt
2 bananas, sliced
1 pint strawberries, hulled and quartered

Directions
1. Prepare the granola. In a cast iron skillet over medium heat, melt the coconut oil.
2. Add the rolled oats and stir to coat. Cook, stirring often, until they begin to brown.
3. Add the brown sugar and cinnamon and mix well. Cook another minute or so.
4. In your for serving dishes, layer a few slices of banana and some strawberries.
5. Spoon on half a cup of yogurt and then a quarter cup of granola.
6. Repeat the layers and serve.

Lunch: Black Bean Wraps

Simple flavors combine to win the day in this bistro-quality meatless lunch.

Serves 4

Ingredients
4 (10-inch) whole wheat tortillas
1 cup salsa
1 cup black beans
1 cup corn
1 avocado chopped
4 cups baby spinach

Directions
1. Lay out the tortillas. You may warm them briefly in a hot pan if desired.
2. Spoon the salsa in rows along the middle of the tortillas and top with beans, corn, avocado, and greens.
3. Wrap one edge of the bread over the fillings and then fold in the sides. Continue rolling it up. Slice, and serve.

Supper: Dutch Oven Roast Chicken

If you're worried that your campers will never be able to eat all this chicken, don't worry! We're counting on that. Those leftovers will be used in other recipes.

Serves 4

Ingredients
2 tablespoons olive oil
1 white or yellow onion
2 cloves garlic, minced
1 (5-pound) roast chicken, skin removed
Salt and pepper to taste
1 ½ teaspoons Italian seasoning
4 white potatoes
2 cups baby carrots

Directions
1. Heat the Dutch oven over 18 briquettes and melt the butter. Add the onion and cook until it begins to brown, about 5 minutes. Stir in the garlic and cook one more minute. Scrape the vegetables to the sides.
2. Sprinkle the chicken with salt, pepper, and the Italian herb blend. Brown it on the top and sides and lift it out of the pot.
3. Pour half a cup of water into the pot and arrange the potatoes and carrots to cover the bottom. Place the chicken on top of the vegetables.
4. Cover the pot and arrange the briquettes so there are 8 under the pot and 16 on top. Try to maintain a medium baking temperature, about 350°F.
5. Cook for two hours, checking the chicken after 1 ½ hours for doneness. It's ready when the internal temperature is 165°F.
6. Set aside half the cooked chicken for later meals, and keep it chilled.

Dessert: Foil Apple Crisp

This all-time favorite needs no introduction! Our recipe is simple and wholesome, and a treat to eat.

Serves 4

Ingredients
⅓ cup oats
½ cup whole wheat flour
½ cup brown sugar
1 teaspoon cinnamon
⅓ cup butter
4 apples, chopped

Directions
1. In a mixing bowl, combine the oats, flour, brown sugar, cinnamon, and butter. Stir with a fork until the mixture is uniform and crumbly. Stir in the apples.
2. Lay out one large piece of foil and fill it with the mixture. Fold to seal.
3. Place the packet on the grill away from direct heat and cook for about 20 minutes, turning once.

DAY TWO RECIPES

Breakfast: Blueberry Chia Pudding

This simple breakfast has lots of protein and fiber to keep you going, and it's both vegan and gluten free.

Serves 4

Ingredients
1 cup chia seeds
4 cups sweetened almond milk (or your choice of milk)
2 tablespoons maple syrup
1 cup fresh blueberries

Directions
1. In a mixing bowl, combine the chia seeds with the milk and maple syrup and mix well. (Individual mason jars can also be used.)
2. Let the mixture sit for five minutes and then stir again. Chill for 1–2 hours, or overnight.
3. Serve with a portion of fresh blueberries.

Lunch: Chicken Salad Lettuce Wraps

Did you know that many store-bought mayo and whipped dressings contain harmful preservatives, and they're loaded with fat? In this recipe we're subbing in some wholesome Greek yogurt as a substitute. Your family will love the taste.

Serves 4

Ingredients
4 cups shredded chicken (or half of the leftover chicken)
2 stalks celery, diced
1 apple, chopped
1 cup Greek yogurt
Salt and pepper to taste
4 leaves Bibb lettuce (or Romaine)

Directions
1. Combine the chicken, celery, apple, yogurt, salt, and pepper, and stir to combine.
2. Rinse the lettuce leaves and pat them dry. Spoon a portion of the salad onto each leaf. Wrap, and serve.

Supper: Shrimp and Wild Rice

This easy, tasty, and low-calorie supper cooks up in one pan.

Serves 4

Ingredients
2 tablespoons butter
1 white or yellow onion
1 cup mushrooms, sliced
2 cups long grain and wild rice blend (unseasoned)
Salt and pepper to taste
2 ½ cups water
1 pound large or jumbo shrimp (thawed, ready to cook)
1 cup snow peas, trimmed and chopped

Directions
1. In a Dutch oven or skillet, melt the butter and cook the onion until it is translucent. Stir in the mushrooms and cook another 3–4 minutes, until the mixture begins to brown.
2. Add the dry rice and let it cook with the vegetables and butter until it is lightly browned, about 3 minutes. Stir often and don't let it burn. Season with salt and pepper.
3. Add the water and bring the mixture to a boil. Cover the pot and let it simmer for 15 minutes, and then stir in the shrimp and snow peas.
4. Cook for an additional 8–10 minutes, uncovered, until the shrimp is pink and the rice and peas are tender.

Dessert: No Bake Chocolate Oat Bars

The kids can make this while you prepare supper! Feel free to experiment by adding your own favorite ingredients.

Serves 4-8

Ingredients
1 cup rolled oats
¾ cup shredded, unsweetened coconut
⅓ cup mini chocolate chips
½ cup almond butter
⅓ cup maple syrup

Directions
1. In a large mixing bowl, combine all the ingredients.
2. Spoon the mixture into a 9x9 baking pan and gently press it down.
3. Let it set for 10–15 minutes in a cool place, and then cut it into 8 pieces.

DAY THREE RECIPES

Breakfast: Turkey Bacon and Spinach Frittata

This simple paleo breakfast will please everyone at your table.

Serves 4

Ingredients
1 pound turkey bacon
1 tablespoon coconut oil
1 ½ cups baby spinach
8 eggs
½ cup 2% milk
4 ounces Feta cheese, crumbled

Directions
1. In a cast iron pan over medium heat, cook the turkey bacon in the oil until crisp. Set aside half the bacon (cooled and chilled) and chop the rest.
2. Place the chopped bacon back in the pan and add the spinach. Cook until it wilts but is still bright.
3. Meanwhile, whisk the eggs with the milk.
4. When the spinach is ready, pour the egg mixture into the pan. Spread everything out evenly and move the pan to medium-low heat.
5. Dot the surface of the frittata with cheese. Cover with foil and cook until the eggs are set, about 10 minutes.

Lunch: Chicken Corn Chowder

Comfort food to the rescue! We forego the heavy cream in favor of some protein-packed chicken. You won't even miss it, and your heart will thank you.

Serves 4

Ingredients
¼ cup butter
1 white or yellow onion
1 stalk celery, diced
½ cup baby carrots, diced small
¼ cup all-purpose flour
4 cups 1% milk
2 white potatoes, diced small
1 (12-ounce) can corn
4 cups shredded chicken (or the remaining left over)
Salt and pepper to taste

Directions
1. In a Dutch oven over medium heat, melt the butter. Add the onion, celery, and carrot, and cook until softened.
2. Stir in the flour and cook until begins to brown. Gradually whisk in the milk, stirring to prevent any lumps from forming.
3. Add the potatoes, corn, and chicken. Bring the mixture to a simmer and cook until the potatoes are tender, about 15 minutes.

Supper: Turkey and Chickpea Burgers

With this recipe, we'll prepare extra turkey mixture to use in meatballs for another supper.

Serves 4

Ingredients
2 pounds ground turkey
2 teaspoons salt
2 teaspoons black pepper
2 teaspoons garlic powder
3 tablespoons water
1 (15-ounce) can chickpeas, drained and rinsed
2 tablespoons coconut oil
4 whole wheat hamburger buns
Optional toppings: tomatoes, pickle, lettuce, onion

Directions
1. In a mixing bowl, gently combine the ground turkey with the salt, pepper, garlic powder, and water. Be careful not to over-mix.
2. Remove half the mixture and place it in a tightly sealed bag. Keep it well chilled.
3. In a separate bowl, use a fork to mash the chickpeas to your desired consistency, and stir them into the remaining turkey.
4. Form the turkey mixture into four patties.
5. Place a cast iron pan over medium heat and warm the coconut oil. Brown the patties on both sides and cook to an internal temperature of 165°F.
6. Serve the turkey patties on the buns (toasted, if you like) with your favorite toppings.

Dessert: Lemon Blueberry Biscuits

You can put a little glaze on a fluffy biscuit and that makes it dessert. (It's science, right?) These light, fluffy, and tart biscuits are perfect for tasting (or testing) our hypothesis.

Serves 8

Ingredients
1 cup all-purpose flour
¾ cup whole wheat flour
½ cup white sugar
2 teaspoons baking powder
½ teaspoon baking soda
¼ teaspoon salt
1 cup Greek yogurt
1 egg
¼ cup butter, melted
Zest of half a lemon
1 cup fresh blueberries

Glaze
1 cup icing sugar
Juice of 1 lemon
Zest of half a lemon

Directions
1. Combine the flour, sugar, baking powder, baking soda, and salt. Place the mixture in a resealable bag.
2. Line your Dutch oven with aluminum foil and coat it with cooking spray. Prepare the coals.
3. In a mixing bowl, combine the yogurt, egg, melted butter, and lemon zest.
4. Stir in the dry ingredients until just combined. Gently fold in the blueberries.

5. Spoon the batter by ⅓ cupfuls into the prepared Dutch oven. Put the cover on.
6. Place the oven on 12 coals and arrange 15 coals on top.
7. Bake for 15–20 minutes, until the biscuits are cooked through and golden brown.
8. Meanwhile, prepare the glaze.
9. Drizzle the glaze over the biscuits while they're still warm. Enjoy!

DAY FOUR RECIPES

Breakfast: Breakfast BLT Sandwiches

Let's hope nobody found the leftover turkey bacon in the cooler! We'll use it to make some breakfast BLT sandwiches.

Serves 4

Ingredients
1 tablespoon butter
4 eggs
8 slices turkey bacon (left over)
4 whole wheat hamburger buns
1 tomato, sliced
4 leaves Bibb or Romaine lettuce, torn
Salt and pepper to taste

Directions
1. Heat a cast iron pan over medium heat and melt the butter. Fry the eggs to your liking and move them to the side.
2. Place the turkey bacon slices in the pan with the eggs to warm.
3. Toast the buns, if desired.
4. Assemble the sandwiches with egg, bacon, tomato, lettuce, and salt and pepper.

Lunch: Bean Salad

This fresh and light salad is loaded with fiber, protein, and nutrients. Enjoy a bowl while sitting in the shade!

Serves 6

Ingredients
2 tablespoons olive oil
2 tablespoons white sugar
Juice from 1 lemon
Salt and pepper to taste
1 (15-ounce) can chickpeas, drained and rinsed
1 (15-ounce) can black beans, drained and rinsed
1 (12-ounce) can corn
1 stalk celery, diced
1 tomato, diced
1 red onion, thinly sliced

Directions
1. In a large mixing bowl, combine the oil, sugar, lemon juice, and salt and pepper. Mix well.
2. Add the other ingredients and stir to combine.
3. Let the salad sit for one hour, chilled, to marinate.

Supper: Rosemary and Lime Steak

These steaks are deliciously tart and tender. Set two aside; we have plans for those tomorrow!

Serves 4

Ingredients
4 white potatoes
6 (5-ounce) sirloin steaks
1 teaspoon cracked black pepper
1 teaspoon salt
1 teaspoon garlic powder
2 tablespoons butter, softened
4 small sprigs fresh rosemary
1 lime, sliced
1 white or yellow onion, sliced
1 tablespoon balsamic vinegar

For the salad
6 cups baby spinach
1 red onion, thinly sliced
2 ounces feta cheese, crumbled

For the vinaigrette
2 tablespoons balsamic vinegar
2 tablespoons olive oil
1 tablespoon brown sugar
Salt and pepper to taste

Directions
1. Scrub and pierce the potatoes. Wrap them in foil and place them over indirect heat. Cook, turning occasionally, for 30–45 minutes, until soft.
2. Combine the ingredients for the vinaigrette and set it aside.

3. Meanwhile, lightly grease 6 pieces of foil, 12x12 inches each.
4. Place each steak in the center of a piece of foil, and season them with black pepper, garlic powder, and salt.
5. Spread half a tablespoon of butter onto each steak.
6. Top with rosemary, lime slices, and onions, and drizzle with balsamic vinegar.
7. Fold the foil and place the steaks on the grill.
8. Cook for 20–30 minutes, flipping occasionally, until the internal temperature reaches 145°–165°F, or to taste.
9. Set two of the steaks aside, let them cool, and wrap them tightly. Keep them chilled.
10. Toss the spinach with the onion and feta, and drizzle on the vinaigrette.
11. Serve each steak with a potato and a portion of the salad.

Dessert: Watermelon Pizza

This light dessert is perfect after a steak dinner! The kids love it.

Serves 4

Ingredients
1 small watermelon, sliced like pizza slices
1 cup Greek yogurt
2 kiwis, peeled and chopped
1 banana, sliced
½ cup strawberries
½ cup fresh blueberries

Directions
1. On each watermelon slice, spread some yogurt.
2. Arrange the fruit pieces to make a colorful pizza!
3. Slice, and serve.

DAY FIVE RECIPES

Quinoa Peach Breakfast

This wholesome breakfast is delicious warm, but you can also make it in mason jars at home and keep it in the cooler.

Serves 6

Ingredients
2 cups water
1 cup quinoa
½ teaspoon cinnamon
1 tablespoon coconut oil
Pinch of salt
2 cups plain 2% Greek yogurt
2 large ripe peaches, chopped
¼ cup natural almond butter, divided
4 teaspoons maple syrup, divided

Directions
1. Bring the water to a boil over high heat. Rinse the quinoa and add it to the pot with the cinnamon, coconut oil, and salt.
2. Reduce the heat and simmer until the quinoa is cooked, about 30 minutes.
3. Divide the quinoa into four serving bowls. Top each with half a cup of Greek yogurt, half a chopped peach, a tablespoon of almond butter, and a teaspoon of maple syrup.

Lunch: Steak Quesadillas

Serves 4

Ingredients
4 (10–inch) whole wheat tortillas
10 ounces sirloin steak, sliced (left over)
Salt and pepper to taste
1 red onion, thinly sliced
1 green pepper, thinly sliced
6 ounces Feta cheese

Directions
1. Prepare 4 12-inch squares of foil and grease them lightly.
2. Lay a tortilla on each piece of foil.
3. Divide the ingredients among the tortillas, and fold them over. Fold the foil into a flat packet.
4. Place the packets over medium-low heat and cook, turning once, until crisp and warmed through, about 5 minutes.

Supper: Pineapple Turkey Skewers

Use the rest of the turkey mixture to make these delicious, colorful kebabs that everyone will love!

Serves 4

Ingredients
Turkey mixture (from the burger recipe)
1 green pepper, cut in 1-inch squares
1 orange pepper, cut in 1-inch squares
1 red onion, cut in 1-inch pieces
1 (14-ounce) can pineapple chunks
¼ cup barbecue sauce
1 cup dry quinoa, rinsed

Directions
1. If your skewers are made of bamboo, soak them in water. Preheat a grill over medium heat.
2. Cook the quinoa according to the package instructions.
3. Form the turkey mixture into balls.
4. Alternating vegetables, pineapple, and turkey balls, thread the skewers.
5. Cook over medium heat for 15–20 minutes, turning occasionally. Brush the skewers with barbecue sauce in the second half of cooking. Make sure the turkey is cooked all the way through.
6. Serve the kebabs over a portion of cooked quinoa.

Dessert: Banana Bread

After five days, the rest of those bananas must be reaching peak baking ripeness.

Serves 6

Ingredients
2 large eggs, lightly beaten
3 ripe bananas (about 1 cup mashed)
½ cup Greek yogurt
⅓ cup maple syrup
1 cup all-purpose flour
½ cup whole wheat flour
1 ½ teaspoons baking soda
½ teaspoon salt

Directions
1. Heat a Dutch oven over 18 coals and grease a 9-inch cake pan.
2. In a mixing bowl, beat together the eggs, bananas, yogurt, and maple syrup.
3. Add the dry ingredients and mix just to combine.
4. Pour the batter into the prepared cake pan. Place a few stones or a trivet in the bottom of the Dutch oven, and put in the cake.
5. Arrange the briquettes with 8 underneath, and 12 on top.
6. After 30 minutes, start checking to see if the banana bread is finished. (It's done when a toothpick inserted near the center comes out clean.)

NO FUSS CAMPING MENUS AND RECIPES

NO FUSS 2 DAY-MENU

Day One
Breakfast: Pull Apart French Toasts
Lunch: Pizza on the Vertical
Supper: Chicken Rice with Veggies
Dessert: Apple Cinnamon Buns

Day Two
Breakfast: Easy Camp Cooker Ham 'n Egg Sandwich
Lunch: Chicken and Rice Soup
Supper: Grilled Shrimp and Mushrooms
Dessert: Cherry Cobbler

SHOPPING LIST

Fats
Butter, ¾ cup

Meats and other proteins
Chicken breasts, 6-ounce, 6
Eggs, 6
Ham, deli, 4 slices

Pepperoni, 1 pound
Shrimp, jumbo, 1 ½ pounds

Vegetables and fruits
Apples, Granny Smith, 2
Cherry tomatoes, 16
Mixed vegetables, 12-ounce bag, 1
Mushrooms, cremini, 12
Onion, white, 1
Pepper, green, 1
Potatoes, white, 4

Dairies
Milk, 4 ¼ cups
Cheddar cheese, grated, ½ cup

Grains:
Basmati rice, 1 ½ cups
Bread, 8 slices

Cans
Biscuit dough, refrigerated, 3 cans
Cherry pie filling, 1 can
Cinnamon rolls with icing, 1 can

Seasonings, toppings, others
Brown sugar, 2 tablespoons
Cajun seasoning or seasoned salt, 1 tablespoon
Cinnamon, 2 teaspoons
Italian salad dressing, ¼ cup
Marinara sauce, 1 cup
Pepper
Salt

DAY ONE RECIPES

Breakfast: Pull Apart French Toasts

At home, you might choose to prepare this tasty breakfast using your own biscuit recipe, but here at the campsite we're taking the shortcut.

Serves 4-6

Ingredients
2 cans refrigerated biscuit dough
2 eggs
¼ cup milk
2 teaspoons cinnamon
2 tablespoons brown sugar
2 tablespoons butter

Directions
1. Cut the individual biscuits into four pieces each.
2. In a bowl, combine the eggs, milk, cinnamon, and brown sugar.
3. Add the dough pieces and toss to thoroughly coat. Set aside.
4. Place the butter in the Dutch oven.
5. Prepare your Dutch oven by placing 18 hot coals on the bottom and 6 on top.
6. Empty the contents of the bowl over the melted butter in the Dutch oven and toss to ensure even coverage. Cover with the lid.
7. Add remaining hot coals on the lid.
8. Cook for 25–30 minutes.

Lunch: Pizza on the Vertical

The kids will love cooking their pizza on a stick!

Serves 4

Ingredients

1 pound pepperoni, sliced

1 green bell pepper, seeded and cut in squares

16 cherry tomatoes

1 onion, quartered, slices separated

1 cup prepared marinara sauce

Directions

1. If your skewers are bamboo, soak them in water.
2. Thread the pepperoni and veggies onto the skewers.
3. Cook over an open flame until the veggies get a slight char.
4. Warm the marinara sauce in a saucepan over medium heat for 5–6 minutes, until heated through.
5. Serve skewers with marinara sauce for dipping.

Supper: Chicken Rice with Veggies

This one-pot meal is easy and nutritious.

Serves 4

Ingredients
4 (6-ounce) boneless skinless chicken breasts, cut into chunks
4 tablespoons butter, divided
1 ½ cups Basmati rice
1 tablespoon Cajun seasoning or seasoned salt
3 cups water
1 (12-ounce) bag mixed veggies

Directions
1. Season the chicken with poultry rub.
2. Heat 2 tablespoons of butter in Dutch oven over hot coals or burner.
3. Add the chicken chunks and cook until opaque (about 10 minutes).
4. Transfer the chicken to a plate.
5. Add the remaining butter, rice, seasoning, and water to the Dutch oven. Stir.
6. Bring the mixture to a boil. Cover and let it simmer for 15 minutes.
7. Remove the lid and stir in the chicken and veggies.
8. Replace the lid and cook until the rice has absorbed most of the liquid and the veggies are tender (about 5 minutes).
9. Set aside a third of the mixture and serve the rest. Chill the reserved portion.

Dessert: Apple Cinnamon Buns

Easy, peasy, delicious!

Serves 4

Ingredients

1 tablespoon butter
1 tube large cinnamon rolls with icing
2 Granny Smith apples, peeled, cored and sliced

Directions

1. Place a large cast iron skillet over medium heat and add the butter. When it has melted, swirl the pan to coat the bottom.
2. Unwrap the cinnamon buns and arrange them in the skillet. Slide apple slices between them and in some of the cracks.
3. Cover the pan with a lid or a sheet of aluminum foil. Cook for 15–20 minutes, or until the buns are cooked through.
4. When they're finished, drizzle the icing packets over top.

DAY TWO RECIPES

Breakfast: Easy Camp Cooker Ham 'n Egg Sandwich

Munch on this hassle-free breakfast sandwich in just 10 minutes using only a few simple ingredients.

Serves 4

Ingredients
4 eggs
Salt and pepper, to taste
¼ cup butter, softened
8 slices bread
½ cup cheddar cheese, grated
4 slices deli ham

Directions
1. Melt a little butter in a skillet and fry the eggs to your liking. Set them aside.
2. Divide the remaining butter and spread it on one side of each bread slice.
3. Layer bread, with butter facing outside, a fried egg, cheese, ham, and another bread slice, with butter facing outside.
4. Cook for 5 minutes, or until nicely browned.
5. Repeat for the remaining sandwiches.
6. Serve.

Lunch: Chicken and Rice Soup

Turning a casserole into a soup is one of our favorite leftover hacks!

Serves 4

Ingredients
Leftover chicken mixture from the previous night
4 cups milk

Directions
1. In a medium pot over medium heat, combine the leftover chicken and rice mixture with the milk.
2. Heat until steamy, and serve.

Supper: Grilled Shrimp and Mushrooms

These delicious shrimp and mushroom skewers are so easy and delicious!

Serves 4

Ingredients
1 ½ pounds jumbo shrimp, shelled and deveined
12 Cremini mushrooms
¼ cup Italian salad dressing
4 white potatoes
1 tablespoon butter
Salt and pepper to taste

Directions
1. Combine the shrimp and mushrooms with the salad dressing and let them sit for 1 hour. If your skewers are bamboo, soak them in water.
2. Prepare a 12x18 sheet of aluminum foil and spread the butter on it.
3. Scrub and chop the potatoes. Arrange them on the foil, season with salt and pepper, and fold it closed. Please the packet over medium heat and cook, rotating and flipping from time to time for about 30 minutes.
4. Thread the shrimp and mushrooms onto the skewers.
5. Grill shrimp skewers with mushrooms over medium heat for about 6 minutes, and serve with a portion of the potatoes.

Dessert: Cherry Cobbler

So easy. So gooooood.

Serves 4

Ingredients
1 can cherry pie filling
¼ cup water
1 can refrigerated biscuit dough

Directions
1. Spread the cherry pie filling in a cast iron skillet, and use the water to thin it out a little.
2. Separate the biscuits and cut them in smaller pieces. Scatter the pieces over the cherry filling.
3. Cover the pan with a lid or a sheet of foil and place it on the grill on medium heat.
4. Cook for about 20 minutes, until the filling is bubbly and the biscuit pieces are cooked through and golden.

NO FUSS 3-DAY MENU

Day One
Breakfast: Country Breakfast
Lunch: Cheesy Penne Pasta in a Pot
Supper: Roast Pork Dinner
Dessert: Peachy Mallow Foil Packs

Day Two
Breakfast: Bluberry Pancakes
Lunch: Camp Carnitas
Supper: Campfire Honey Garlic Chicken
Dessert: Blueberry and Pineapple Dump Cake

Day Three
Breakfast: Morning Bread Pudding
Lunch: Cheesy Sausage Soup
Supper: Pulled Pork Sandwiches
Dessert: Moose Farts

SHOPPING LIST

Fats
Butter, ¾ cup
Olive oil, ¼ cup

Meats and other proteins
Chicken breast, boneless skinless, 1 pound

Coconut, shredded unsweetened, 1 ½ cups
Eggs, 12
Pork sausage, 1 pound
Pork butt roast, boneless, 5-6 pounds
Sausages, large, spicy Italian, 2

Vegetables and fruits
Broccoli florets, 2 cups
Carrots, 6-8
Cranberries, dried, ¼ cup
Garlic, 2 cloves
Jalapeño, 1 (optional)
Lettuce, 3 cups
Mushrooms, sliced, 3 cups
Onion, white or yellow, 2
Peaches, 4
Potatoes, white, 4
Potato hash browns, frozen, 2 cups
Spinach, 2 cups
Strawberries, fresh, ½ cup
Tomatoes, 2

Dairies
Cheddar cheese, shredded, 3 ½ cups
Milk, 3 ½ cups
Parmesan, shredded, ½ cup
Whipped cream (canned) 1

Grains
Basmati rice, 1 cup
Bread, white, 8 slices
Graham cracker crumbs, 2 cups
Penne pasta, 3 cups dry
Sandwich buns, 4–6
Tortillas, flour or corn, 4 large or 8 small

Cans

Biscuit dough, 1 can

Blueberries, fresh, ½ cup

Blueberry pie filling, 1 (21-ounce) can

Chicken stock, 2 cups

Lemon-lime soda, 1 can

Peppers, roasted, 1 (10-ounce) jar

Pineapple, crushed, 1 (8-ounce) can

Seasonings, toppings, others

Barbecue sauce, 1 (10-ounce) bottle

Box yellow cake mix (18 ½-ounce), 1

Brown sugar, 2 tablespoons

Chocolate chips, 1 ½ cups

Cinnamon, 1 teaspoon

Gravy mix, brown, 1 packet

Honey Garlic sauce, 1 (10-ounce) bottle

Maple syrup, ½ cup

Marshmallows, mini, 1 cup

Pancake mix, plain, 2 cups

Pepper

Pickles, sweet, ½ cup sliced (optional)

Salsa, ½ cup (optional)

Salt

Sour cream, ½ cup (optional)

Sweetened condensed milk, 1 (14-ounce) can

Taco seasoning, 1 packet

DAY ONE RECIPES

Breakfast: Country Breakfast

This is a very hearty and delicious breakfast recipe to enjoy while camping.

Serves 4

Ingredients
1 pound pork sausage
2 cups frozen hash browns
8 eggs
1 cup cheddar cheese, shredded
1 can refrigerated biscuit dough
Salt and pepper to taste

Directions
1. Place the Dutch oven over hot coals and cook the sausage in it until the meat is golden brown. Drain most of the fat.
2. Spoon or shake the prepared hash browns over the sausage.
3. Crack the eggs over the hash browns and sprinkle on the cheddar cheese.
4. Arrange the biscuits over the cheese.
5. Cover the Dutch oven and place hot coals on the lid.
6. Cook for 45 minutes, or until the eggs are set.

Lunch: Cheesy Penne Pasta in a Pot

Whip up this deliciously flavorful pasta in just 15 minutes. We will make a little bit extra to use another day.

Serves 4

Ingredients
2 tablespoons olive oil
1 onion, chopped
2 cloves garlic, finely chopped
1 cup mushrooms, sliced
3 cups penne pasta, dry
2 cups chicken stock
1 (10-ounce) jar roasted peppers, undrained
2 cups cheddar cheese, shredded
½ cup Parmesan cheese
2 cups fresh spinach

Directions
1. In a Dutch oven over 18 coals, heat the olive oil. Add the onions and cook for 1–2 minutes. Add the garlic and mushrooms. Sauté for 2–5 minutes, until the mushrooms are well browned.
2. Stir in the pasta, chicken stock, and peppers. Cover, bring it to a boil, and cook for about 5–8 minutes, then remove the lid.
3. Add the cheeses and spinach. Continue to cook on low heat, stirring, until the pasta is cooked to your liking.
4. Scoop out a third of the mixture and place it in a sealed container. Keep it chilled.

Supper: Roast Pork Dinner

You'll enjoy every bite of this tender roast pork, and the leftovers will make your life so much easier over the next few days.

Serves 4-6

Ingredients
2 tablespoons olive oil
1 onion, diced
1 (5–6 pound) boneless pork butt roast
Salt and pepper to taste
2 cups water
4 medium potatoes, scrubbed and halved
4–6 carrots
1 packet brown gravy mix

Directions
1. In a Dutch oven over 18 coals, heat the olive oil. Add the onion and cook for 1–2 minutes.
2. Cut the roast into 4-inch chunks and season them with salt and pepper. Brown them in the Dutch oven.
3. Pour the water into the pot and add the potatoes and carrots.
4. Cover the pot and place it over medium heat. Let it simmer (the temperature should be about 325°F) for 1 ½–2 hours, or until the meat is very tender.
5. Use a slotted spoon to remove the meat and vegetables from the pot. Skim off any excess grease and stir in the gravy powder. (Add more water if needed.)
6. Set aside a little more than half the meat (there will be plenty!) and serve the rest with gravy, potatoes, and carrots.
7. Chill the unused meat and keep it cold.

Dessert: Peachy Mallow Foil Packs

Melt-in-your mouth delicious!

Serves 4

Ingredients
4 peaches
4 tablespoons butter
1 teaspoon cinnamon
1 cup mini marshmallows
½ cup fresh blueberries
½ cup fresh strawberries, sliced

Directions
1. Prepare 4 heavy-duty aluminum foil sheets.
2. Slice the peaches and gently separate them from the pit. Place each peach on a piece of foil.
3. Into the center of the peach, place a tablespoon of butter and a sprinkle of cinnamon.
4. Add two tablespoons of marshmallows and a few blueberries and strawberries.
5. Close the foil around the fruit, leaving a little space on the top so it doesn't stick.
6. Arrange the peaches near the coals for about 5 minutes, until they are heated through and the marshmallows are gooey.

DAY TWO RECIPES

Breakfast: Bluberry Pancakes

This is an easy way to quickly jazz up jazz up classic camp pancakes.

Serves 4–6

Ingredients
2 cups pancake mix, plain
Water, for mixing
2 tablespoons butter
½ (21-ounce) can blueberry pie filling* (or ½ cup fresh blueberries)
1 cup (canned) whipped cream, for topping

Directions
1. Combine the pancake mix with enough water to make the desired consistency.
2. Heat a skillet over the fire or grill.
3. Melt some of the butter and pour in a scoop of batter. Cook until bubbles appear, and then flip it over. Repeat with more butter and batter until it's all used.
4. Serve with pie filling and whipped cream. Chill the remaining pie filling.

*Note: we will be using the other half of the can in the dessert recipe for the Blueberry and Pineapple Dump Cake.

Lunch: Camp Carnitas

A portion of our leftover pork will make a delicious filling for our lunch carnitas. With a sprinkle of seasoning and a handful of fresh vegetables, it won't feel at all like a repeat.

Serves 4–6

Ingredients
1 pound leftover pork roast
2 tablespoons butter
1 packet taco seasoning
½ cup water
4 large or 8 small tortillas, corn or flour
2 cups lettuce, torn
1 tomato, diced
1 jalapeño, sliced (optional)
½ cup each salsa and sour cream, for serving (optional)

Directions
1. In a skillet over medium heat, melt the butter.
2. Shred the pork with two forks, and cook it in the butter until it's crisp.
3. Sprinkle on the taco seasoning and enough water to moisten. Let it simmer about 5 minutes.
4. Serve the meat mixture on the tortillas with all your favorite toppings!

Supper: Campfire Honey Garlic Chicken

Honey garlic is a classic flavor combination that everyone can get behind. Bottled sauce makes it a total breeze to make.

Serves 4 6

Ingredients

2 tablespoons butter
1 pound boneless chicken breast, sliced
2 cups mushrooms, sliced
2 carrots, peeled and thinly sliced
2 cups broccoli florets
1 (10-ounce) bottle honey garlic sauce
2 cups water
1 cup basmati rice

Directions

1. In a cast iron pan, melt the butter over medium-high heat and brown the chicken,
2. Add the mushrooms and cook until they begin to brown.
3. Meanwhile, in a separate pot, boil the water and cook the rice.
4. Add the carrots and broccoli to the chicken mixture. Cover, and cook about 5 minutes, until they begin to wilt.
5. Pour the honey garlic sauce over the chicken and vegetable mixture. Add water to make more sauce, if needed.
6. Serve the chicken and vegetables over a portion of the rice.

Dessert: Blueberry and Pineapple Dump Cake

With just a few ingredients you can prepare a delicious camp dessert.

Serves 8-10

Ingredients

½ (21–ounce) can blueberry pie filling (left from breakfast)
1 (8–ounce) can crushed pineapple
1 (18 ½–ounce) box yellow cake mix
1 can lemon-lime soda

Directions

1. Heat the coals until white.
2. Line the Dutch oven with aluminum foil and spray it with nonstick cooking spray.
3. Mix the pie filling with the pineapple until well blended. Scoop the mixture into the Dutch oven.
4. In a bowl, stir together boxed cake mix with the soda. Pour the batter into the Dutch oven, over the pie filling.
5. Cover. Arrange the pot with 8 coals underneath and 12 on top.
6. Bake until the cake is fragrant and a toothpick comes out clean when pierced at center of cake, about 20–25 minutes.
7. Carefully remove the cake from the Dutch oven. Let it cool before serving.
8. Chill the remaining pie filling.

DAY THREE RECIPES

Breakfast: Morning Bread Pudding

This classic breakfast cooks up with very little mess, and everyone will love it.

Serves 4

Ingredients
8 slices white bread, cubed
¼ cup dried cranberries
4 large eggs, beaten
½ cup milk
2 tablespoons brown sugar
½ cup maple syrup

Directions
1. Coat a piece of heavy-duty foil with oil and gently shape the edges to form a shallow bowl. Put in the bread and cranberries.
2. Beat the eggs with the milk and sugar. Pour the mixture over the bread. Wait a few minutes before cooking for the egg mixture to be absorbed into the bread.
3. Fold the foil to make a tent packet.
4. Cook for approximately 12–15 minutes, or until set and cooked through. Let rest a few minutes before serving with syrup.

Lunch: Cheesy Sausage Soup

Toss in some spicy sausage and milk, and our leftover pasta becomes a hearty soup for lunch.

Serves 4

Ingredients
2 large spicy Italian sausages
3 cups milk
Leftover Cheesy Penne Pasta
½ cup shredded cheddar cheese

Directions
1. Heat a Dutch oven over 18 coals.
2. Slice the sausages into rounds and brown them in the pot. Drain any excess grease, but leave some for flavor.
3. Add the milk and leftover pasta, and stir to combine. Cook over medium heat until it is heated through and steamy.
4. Serve with a sprinkle of shredded cheddar.

Supper: Pulled Pork Sandwiches

Tonight, we'll use up the rest of that pulled pork in our mouth-watering pulled pork sandwiches.

Serves 4

Ingredients
2 pounds leftover pork roast
1 (10-ounce) bottle barbecue sauce
4–6 sandwich buns

Optional toppings:
1 cup lettuce, torn
1 tomato, sliced
½ cup sweet pickles, sliced

Directions
1. Shred the pork using two forks.
2. Heat a cast iron pan over medium heat.
3. In the pan, combine the shredded meat with the barbecue sauce, and heat until bubbly.
4. Serve a portion of the meat on the sandwich buns, together with the toppings of your choice.

Dessert: Moose Farts

Sorry. That's what they're called. Appropriate for camping, right?

Yields 40 Moose Farts

Ingredients
1 (14-ounce) can sweetened condensed milk
¼ cup butter, melted
1 ½ cups coconut flakes
1 ½ cups graham cracker crumbs, plus a little for coating
1 ½ cups chocolate chips

Directions
1. Combine the sweetened condensed milk with the melted butter.
2. Add the coconut, graham crumbs, and chocolate chips, and mix well.
3. Set the mixture aside in a cool place for an hour, and then roll it into balls about 1 inch in diameter. Roll each ball in graham cracker crumbs to coat. (Makes about 40 balls.)
4. Store in a cool place until firm.

NO FUSS 5-DAY MENU

Day One
Breakfast: Orange Sticky Buns
Lunch: Cornbread Fritters
Supper: Glazed Spiral Ham Dinner
Dessert: Classic Banana Boats

Day Two
Breakfast: Bacon and Egg Protein Packs
Lunch: Dutch Oven Pizza
Supper: Chicken Pot Pie
Dessert: Pumpkin Pie Cake

Day Three
Breakfast: Ham and Onion Crescent Wraps
Lunch: Ramen Bowls
Supper: Beef Tacos
Dessert: One Pan Cookie Pizza

Day Four
Breakfast: Easy Apple Caramel Monkey Bread
Lunch: Campfire Nachos
Supper: Ham and Broccoli Mac and Cheese
Dessert: Campfire Fondue

Day Five
Breakfast: Bacon Raspberry Pancakes
Lunch: Apple Chicken Grilled Wraps
Supper: One Pot Beef Stroganoff
Dessert: 6-minute Camping Éclairs

Shopping List

Fats
Butter, ½ cup
Cooking spray
Vegetable oil, ¾ cup

Meats and other proteins
Bacon, 16 slices
Beef, ground, 2 pounds
Chicken, rotisserie, 3 pounds (meat only)
Eggs, 10
Ham, spiralized 4–5 pounds, 1
Pepperoni, pizza, 15–20 slices
Strip steak, 1 pound

Vegetables and fruits
Apples, Granny Smith, 5
Bananas, large, 6
Broccoli florets, 3 cups
Cabbage, small, 1
Carrots, 5
Lettuce, shredded, 1 cup
Oranges, large, 3
Onion, green, 1 bunch
Onion, red, 1
Onion, white, 1
Pepper, green, ½ (optional)
Potato hash browns, frozen, 2 cups
Potatoes, white, 4
Raspberries, 1 cup

Strawberries, 2 cups
Tomatoes, cherry, 1 cup
Tomatoes, 2
Vegetable mix, frozen, 1 (12-ounce) bag

Dairies
Cheddar cheese, shredded, 7 ½ cups
Mozzarella cheese, shredded, 2 ¾ cups
Milk, 3 cups
Sour cream, 2 cups

Grains
Cornbread mix, 2 cups
Corn tortilla chips, 1 bag
Egg noodles, wide, 1 pound
Flour tortillas, 10- or 12-inch, 10
Pancake mix, 2 cups
Pizza dough, frozen, 1 medium
Macaroni, elbow, dry, 1 pound
Ramen noodles, 4 packets

Cans:
Beef broth, 1 ½ cups
Biscuit dough, (large biscuits) refrigerated, 4 cans
Cookie dough, prepared, 1 can (tube)
Corn, 1 can
Crescent roll dough, refrigerated, 2 cans
Mushrooms, 3 (6-ounce) cans
Pizza sauce, 1 (6-ounce) can

Seasonings, toppings, others
Cake mix, Spice, 1 box
Caramel syrup, 2 cups
Chocolate chips, 1 ¼ cups
Chocolate frosting, 6 tablespoons

Cream of chicken soup, 2 cans
Lemon soda, ½ can
Marshmallows, mini, ½ cup
Marshmallows, regular, 8
Mustard, Dijon, 2 tablespoons
Pepper
Pudding, vanilla, snack-sized cups, 6
Pumpkin purée, 1 (15-ounce) can
Salsa, 1 cup, 1 cup
Salt
Sugar, white, 2 tablespoons
Sweetened condensed milk, 1 (14-ounce) can
Taco seasoning, 2 packets
Whipped cream, 1 can

DAY ONE RECIPES

Breakfast: Orange Sticky Buns

Sticky buns are a classic breakfast treat. The following recipe has a slight twist, though. Cooking in an orange hull makes these easy to eat and clean up, and they're certainly a unique experience!

Serves 4–6

Cooking Techniques: foil packets placed on a grate directly on the coals, on the grill or a camping propane/gas barbecue

Ingredients
1 package refrigerated biscuits (6 large biscuits)
3 large oranges, halved and hulled (save the flesh for snacking)
½ cup caramel syrup
Cooking spray

Directions
1. Spray 6 heavy-duty foil aluminum sheets with cooking spray.
2. Drizzle a little caramel in the bottom of each orange shell.
3. Quarter the biscuits and place 4 pieces in each orange shell. Drizzle with more caramel.
4. Place orange halves on the foil sheets and fold, leaving enough place for the buns to rise. Place the oranges on a grate placed directly on the coals. Cook for about 15 minutes, watching progress carefully*.

*NOTE: You may have to place oranges above the coals/ fire on a baking sheet to allow them to rise as they bake.

Lunch: Cornbread Fritters

No time for anything too involved? This lunch is quick and satisfying.

Serves 4–6

Ingredients
2 cups cornbread mix
2 tablespoons sugar
½ cup water
½ cup canned corn, drained (save the other half)
¼ cup vegetable oil, for frying

Directions
1. Tip the cornbread mix and sugar into a bowl and whisk in the water. Do not overmix.
2. Fold in the corn.
3. Heat a cast iron pan over medium-high heat and warm a few tablespoons of oil until it is quite hot.
4. Spoon in some of the batter and cook until browned, about 3 minutes.
5. Flip, and cook on the other side.
6. Repeat until all the fritters are done.

Supper: Glazed Spiral Ham Dinner

Oh yes, you can! It's super easy to cook ham over the fire; in fact, it requires almost no work at all. And you can use the leftover for another meal!

Serves 4–6

Ingredients

1 (4–5-pound) spiralized ham
2 cups water
4 medium white potatoes, scrubbed
1 small cabbage
4 medium carrots
¼ cup caramel sauce

Directions

1. Place the ham in the Dutch oven with the water. Cover, and cook over 8 coals (with 12 coals on the lid) for about 1 hour.
2. Cut the cabbage into 6 wedges. Set one aside for a later recipe.
3. Add the potatoes, remaining cabbage, and carrots to the pot. Cook for 45 minutes.
4. Drizzle the caramel sauce over the ham, cover, and cook 15 minutes,
5. Wrap and chill the leftovers as they will be used in Day 4 for the Ham and Broccoli Mac and Cheese.

Dessert: Classic Banana Boats

Let's begin with a classic! These gooey sweet treats are a guaranteed crowd pleaser.

Serves 4

Ingredients
4 large bananas
½ cup chocolate chips
½ cup mini marshmallows

Directions
1. Slice each (unpeeled) banana lengthwise, and gently pry it open.
2. Into the center, place some chocolate chips and marshmallows.
3. Wrap the filled bananas in foil, and place them near the hot coals for 5–7 minutes.
4. A grown-up should open the foil, because the filling can be quite hot.

DAY TWO RECIPES

Breakfast: Bacon and Egg Protein Packs

These foil breakfast packs are fully customizable and are always delicious. Substitute sausage, ham, peppers, cheese—whatever you like!

Serves 4

Ingredients
8 slices bacon
2 cups hash brown potatoes, thawed
4 eggs
Salt and pepper to taste
1 cup cherry tomatoes
½ cup cheddar cheese, shredded
½ cup green onion, chopped

Directions
1. Cut 4 pieces of foil, about 18 inches long, and fold them into a boat shape to hold the ingredients.
2. Place 2 slices of bacon on each piece of foil and layer on a portion of the hash browns.
3. Crack an egg over the hash browns in each packet and season with salt and pepper to taste.
4. Add the cherry tomatoes, cheddar, and green onion, and fold the packets closed with a little room for steam.
5. Place the packets on the grill over medium heat and cook for about 15–20 minutes, until the bacon and eggs are cooked.

Lunch: Dutch Oven Pizza

Who doesn't love pizza? And your Dutch oven is a great place to cook one.

Serves 4

Ingredients
Prepared pizza dough (medium)
1 (6-ounce) can pizza sauce
15–20 slices pepperoni
½ green pepper, sliced (optional)
½ red onion, sliced
2 cups shredded mozzarella

Directions
1. Heat a Dutch oven over 18 coals and coat it lightly with oil.
2. Form the dough into a circle, and carefully spread it in the bottom of the Dutch oven.
3. Cover and cook for about 5 minutes.
4. Spread the sauce on the dough, being careful not to use too much.
5. Layer on half the mozzarella, then the rest of your toppings, finishing with the rest of the mozzarella.
6. Cover the pot and place some coals on top. It should be ready after about 10 minutes.

Supper: Chicken Pot Pie

A rotisserie chicken and a few easy ingredients make this meal a cinch to prepare.

Serves 4

Ingredients
2 pounds rotisserie chicken, shredded
2 cans condensed cream of chicken soup
1 small can sliced mushrooms
1 cup milk
1 (12-ounce) bag mixed vegetables
1 can refrigerated biscuit dough

Directions
1. Prepare a large skillet with a light coat of cooking spray.
2. In the pan, mix the chicken, condensed soup, mushrooms, milk, and vegetables. Spread the mixture over the bottom of the pot.
3. Warm the pan until the mixture just begins to bubble. Give it a little stir.
4. Separate the biscuits and arrange them on the filling. Cover the pan loosely with foil and place it on medium-low heat. Continue cooking for 15–30 more minutes, until the biscuits are cooked through.

Dessert: Pumpkin Pie Cake

Surprise the campers with this this unique twist on pumpkin pie.

Serves 10

Ingredients
1 (15-ounce) can pumpkin purée
1 (14-ounce) can sweetened condensed milk
2 eggs
1 box spice cake mix
½ can lemon soda

You need: parchment paper

Directions
1. Prepare the charcoal.
2. Line the Dutch oven with parchment paper and lightly coat it with nonstick spray.
3. Mix the pumpkin purée, sweetened condensed milk, and eggs in a large mixing bowl.
4. Pour this mixture into the Dutch oven and sprinkle the cake mix on top.
5. Carefully pour the soda over the cake mix.
6. Place the lid on the Dutch oven. Place it on 8 coals, with 16 coals on the lid.
7. Bake for 45 minutes and check for doneness. If a butter knife inserted in the center comes out clean, it's ready.
8. Remove the Dutch oven from the coals and enjoy!

DAY THREE RECIPES

Breakfast: Ham and Onion Crescent Wraps

These tasty bundles are fun for the kids to make and eat!

Serves 4

Ingredients
1 can refrigerated crescent roll dough
½ pound leftover ham
½ red onion, sliced
¾ cup mozzarella cheese, shredded
2 tablespoons Dijon mustard

Directions
1. Packet fold style: Tent
2. Grease 4 12"x12" or larger heavy-duty aluminum foil sheets with cooking spray.
3. In the center of each piece of aluminum foil, arrange two pieces of crescent dough.
4. Top each one with a portion of ham, red onion, cheese, and Dijon mustard.
5. Roll each crescent, crimping to secure.
6. Create a tent style fold with each packet and place them on your heat source.
7. Cook for 20 minutes, or until the crescents are cooked through.

Lunch: Ramen Bowls

Quick, salty, and satisfying, this ramen soup always hits the spot.

Serves 4

Ingredients
4 servings ramen noodles with flavor packets
8 cups water
4 eggs
8 ounces rotisserie chicken, shredded
1 carrot, finely shredded
1/6 small cabbage (set aside from the ham dinner), finely shredded

Directions
1. Rinse the eggs under cold water.
2. Boil the eggs in the water. After 3 minutes or so, add the ramen noodles as well, but not the flavor packets.
3. When the eggs have boiled for 8 minutes, spoon them out of the water and set them aside. Add the flavor packets to the broth.
4. When the noodles have cooked, divide them among four serving bowls. Peel and slice the eggs, placing two halves in each bowl.
5. Add some chicken, carrot, and cabbage to each bowl, and serve.

Supper: Beef Tacos

Tacos for supper! Your campers will think they're in heaven.

Serves 4

Ingredients
2 pounds ground beef
2 packets taco seasoning
½ cup water
4–6 flour tortillas

Toppings:
1 cup lettuce, shredded
2 tomatoes, diced
1 cup cheddar cheese, shredded
1 cup salsa
1 cup sour cream

Directions
1. Heat a cast iron pan and coat it lightly with oil.
2. Brown the meat, breaking it up with the spoon as you go. Drain any excess grease.
3. Mix in the taco seasoning and water. Bring it to a simmer and cook for 10 minutes or so.
4. Scoop out a third of the meat and set it aside. Keep it cold for a later recipe.
5. Warm the tortillas over the grill or in a lightly buttered pan.
6. To assemble the tacos, add some of the beef and top with your favorite toppings, and enjoy!

Dessert: One Pan Cookie Pizza

Who says you can't make cookies at camp? Whip up this delicious all-time favorite dessert with a grill, cast iron pan, and a few ingredients.

Serves 8

Ingredients
1 package refrigerated chocolate chip cookie dough
1–2 cups (canned) whipped cream
¼ cup caramel sauce

Directions
1. Set camping grill to 350°F.
2. Spread the cookie dough in a cast iron pan and place it on the grill.
3. Cover and cook for about 20 minutes until cooked through and golden brown around the edges.
4. Remove it from the heat and let it cool for a few minutes.
5. Top with whipped cream and a drizzle of caramel sauce.

DAY FOUR RECIPES

Breakfast: Easy Apple Caramel Monkey Bread

There might be leftovers of this scrumptious breakfast...but then again, there might not.

Serves 4-6

Ingredients
2 cans biscuit dough
2 Granny Smith apples, diced
¼ cup butter, melted
½ cup caramel sauce

Directions
1. Prepare a Dutch oven over medium heat, about 18 coals. Coat the inside with cooking spray or oil.
2. Open and separate the biscuits. Cut them into quarters.
3. In the pot, layer biscuit pieces with one chopped apple and a drizzle of melted butter and caramel sauce. Repeat the layers and cover the pot.
4. Place 8 coals under the pot and 12 on top. Cook for 20-30 minutes, until the biscuit pieces are cooked through.

Lunch: Campfire Nachos

This big pot of cheesy nachos uses the remaining taco meat from last night.

Serves 4

Ingredients
1 tablespoon vegetable oil
1 bag corn tortilla chips
1 cup salsa, excess liquid drained
2 cups cheddar cheese, shredded
Leftover taco meat

Directions
1. Grease a large Dutch oven with oil.
2. Layer half the chips into the oven.
3. Top the chips with half the salsa, half the cheese, and half the meat.
4. Repeat the steps for the second layer.
5. Cover the Dutch oven with the lid, and place it over your campfire for about 10 minutes.
6. Serve when it's hot and the cheese is melted.

Supper: Ham and Broccoli Mac and Cheese

The last of our ham gets a new flavor partner in this easy mac and cheese entrée.

Serves 4–6

Ingredients
1 pound elbow macaroni
3 cups broccoli florets
1 ½ cups milk
2 cups cheddar cheese, grated
1 pound leftover ham (or what remains)
½ can corn (left over)

Directions
1. Cook the macaroni according to the package directions. In the final 5 minutes, add the broccoli to cook in the water.
2. Drain the pot and place it back over the heat.
3. Add the milk and cheese, and stir until the cheese melts.
4. Stir in the ham and corn, and cook to heat through.

Dessert: Campfire Fondue

This is everyone's absolute favorite. Customize with the dippables you like the most.

Serves 4

Ingredients
⅓ cup milk
¾ cup chocolate chips
8 regular marshmallows

For dipping
2 bananas, cut into chunks
2 Granny Smith apples, cored and cut in chunks
2 cups strawberries, hulled

Directions
1. Pour the milk into a small pot and place it over the coals.
2. Heat with continuous stirring until slightly frothy at edges (about 5 minutes). Make sure not to scorch the milk.
3. Remove the pot from the heat and add the chocolate.
4. Stir until smooth. Place at edge of campfire to keep warm (not hot).
5. Toast marshmallows and fruit, dip into fondue, and enjoy.

DAY FIVE RECIPES

Breakfast: Bacon Raspberry Pancakes

Trust us on this one!

Serves 4–6

Ingredients
8 slices bacon
2 cups pancake mix, plain
Water, for mixing
1 cup fresh raspberries
2 tablespoons butter
1 cup (canned) whipped cream, for topping
⅓ cup caramel syrup, for drizzling

Directions
1. Cook the bacon over medium heat until crisp. Remove it from the heat, cool, and crumble.
2. Combine the pancake mix with enough water to make the desired consistency. Gently fold in the bacon and the raspberries.
3. Heat a skillet over the fire or grill.
4. Melt some of the butter and pour in a scoop of batter. Cook until bubbles appear and then flip it over. Repeat with more butter and batter until it's all used.
5. Serve with whipped cream and a drizzle of syrup.

Lunch: Apple Chicken Grilled Wraps

Apple and cheddar are lovely together. Let's cook some up with chicken in these crispy and nutritious wraps.

Serves 4

Ingredients

4 large flour tortillas

2 tablespoons butter

8 ounces rotisserie chicken

1 cup cheddar cheese, shredded

1 Granny Smith apple, sliced

Directions

1. Lay out 4 12-inch squares of foil and place a tortilla on each.
2. Butter the tortillas and flip them over.
3. Arrange a portion of the chicken, cheddar, and apple on each piece of foil. Fold the edges of the tortilla in, and roll them up. Wrap the foil around them.
4. Place the foil packets near a gentle heat souce and cook for about 10 minutes, turning occasionally. They're ready when the bread is crisp and the cheese is melted.

Supper: One Pot Beef Stroganoff

The hearty aromas of beef and mushroom bring all the hungry bellies to the table for this easy, one-pot meal.

Serves 4

Ingredients
1 pound strip steak, sliced into bite-sized pieces
2 tablespoons vegetable oil
1 onion, diced
2 cans mushrooms
1 ½ cups beef broth
1 pound wide egg noodles
1 cup sour cream

Directions
1. Warm the oil in a cast iron skillet over medium-high heat. Sear the steak slices until they are nice and brown. Remove them to a bowl and cover them with foil.
2. Add the onion and mushrooms to the skillet and cook for a few minutes.
3. Pour in the broth and bring it to a boil. Move the pan to lower heat, add the noodles, and cook until tender.
4. Add a little of the hot broth to the sour cream and mix well. You want to warm up the sour cream so it doesn't curdle in the pot.
5. Add the sour cream mixture to the noodles, and stir in the beef. Cook to heat through, and serve.

Dessert: 6-minute Camping Éclairs

You won't believe how simple this version of the classic French dessert is to make. And it only takes all of 6 minutes, too!

Serves 4–6

Ingredients
¼ cup vegetable oil
1 tube refrigerated crescent rolls, cut into 6 squares
6 snack pack-sized vanilla pudding cups
6 tablespoons chocolate frosting
Whipped cream

Directions
1. Brush the ends of wooden sticks or dowels with oil, then attach each crescent roll square onto each wooden stick by coiling it around the end. Lightly press the end of the dough onto the overlapping dough to secure it in place.
2. Toast the dough over hot coals, rotating to make sure they cook evenly, until lightly brown and a bit crisp.
3. Remove the sticks from the heat and gently pull the cooked dough from the sticks. When cooled, cut them in half, but not the whole way through. Fill the insides with vanilla pudding. Spread chocolate frosting on top and add a dollop of whipped cream.

VEGETARIAN CAMPING MENUS AND RECIPES

VEGETARIAN 2-DAY MENU

Day One
Breakfast: Quinoa Peach Breakfast
Lunch: Lemon and Garlic Portabella Mushrooms
Supper: Cauliflower and Chickpea Curry
Dessert: Dutch Oven Berry Cobbler

Day Two
Breakfast: Vegetarian Croissant Sandwiches
Lunch: Campfire Cheese and Veggies Quesadilla
Supper: Dutch Oven Style Risotto
Dessert: Grilled S'mores Cones

SHOPPING LIST

Fats
Butter, 5 tablespoons, 2 tablespoons
Coconut oil, 1 tablespoon, 3 tablespoons
Olive oil, 2 tablespoons

Proteins
Almond butter, ¼ cup

Vegetables and fruits
Avocado, 1
Berries, mixed, 5 cups
Cauliflower, 1 medium
Corn kernels, ½ cup
Garlic, 7 cloves,
Ginger, 1 1-inch thumb
Lemon, 1
Mushrooms, portabella, 1 pound
Mushrooms, button, 10
Onion, red, 1 small
Onion, white, 1
Peaches, 2
Tomato, 1
Spinach, 1 cup

Dairies
Greek yogurt, plain, 2 cups
Parmesan cheese, 1 cup
Pepper Jack cheese, Provolone cheese, 4 slices

Grains
Croissant, bakery, 1
Quinoa, 1 cup, ½ cup
Rice, arborio, 1 cup
Tortillas, 10-inch, flour, 4
Waffle cones, 6

Cans
Chickpeas (15-ounce) can, 1
Coconut milk, (14-ounce) can, 1
Tomatoes, diced, (14 ½-ounce) can, 1
Vegetable stock, 5 cups

Seasonings, toppings, others

Baking powder, 2 teaspoons
Cornstarch, 2 tablespoons
Chocolate chips, 1 cup
Cinnamon, 1 ¼ teaspoons
Curry powder, 1 ½ tablespoons*
Cumin, 1 teaspoon*
Flour, all-purpose, 1 ½ cups
Honey, ¼ cup
Italian seasoning, 1 teaspoon, 1 tablespoon
Pepper
Marshmallows, mini, 2 cups
Salt
Sugar, white, ½ cup, 1/3 cup
Turmeric, 1 teaspoon*
Wine, white, ½ cup

*Can be combined at home

DAY ONE RECIPES

Breakfast: Quinoa Peach Breakfast

This wholesome breakfast is delicious warm, but you can also make it in mason jars at home and keep it in the cooler.

Serves 4

Ingredients
2 cups water
1 cup quinoa
½ teaspoon cinnamon
1 tablespoon coconut oil
Pinch of salt
2 cups plain Greek yogurt
2 large ripe peaches, chopped
4 tablespoons natural almond butter, divided
4 teaspoons honey, divided

Directions
1. Bring the water to a boil over high heat. Rinse the quinoa and add it to the pot with the cinnamon, coconut oil, and salt.
2. Reduce the heat and simmer until the quinoa is cooked, about 30 minutes.
3. Divide the quinoa into four serving bowls. Top each with half a cup of Greek yogurt, half a chopped peach, a tablespoon of almond butter, and a teaspoon of honey.

Lunch: Lemon and Garlic Portabella Mushrooms

Serves 4

Ingredients
1 pound portabella mushrooms, sliced
1 lemon, sliced
4 cloves garlic, minced
2 tablespoons olive oil
Salt and pepper to taste

Directions
1. Packet fold style: Tent
2. Grease 1 24"x24" heavy-duty aluminum foil with cooking spray.
3. In a large bowl combine the portabella mushrooms, minced garlic, olive oil, salt and cracked black pepper.
4. Transfer the mushrooms to the center of the aluminum foil and top with sliced lemons.
5. Create a tent style fold and add to your heat source.
6. Cook for 20-25 minutes, or until mushrooms are tender.

Prep Tip: This dish can be prepared and packaged at home before heading to the campsite.

Supper: Cauliflower and Chickpea Curry

This recipe is loaded with antioxidants, fiber, and lots of vitamins and minerals. Oh, and it's also delicious.

Serves 4

Ingredients
2 tablespoons coconut oil
1 large onion, diced
3 cloves garlic, minced
1-inch thumb ginger, peeled and minced
1 ½ tablespoons curry powder
1 teaspoon ground cumin
1 teaspoon ground turmeric
1 (15-ounce) cans chickpeas, drained and rinsed
1 (14½ -ounce) can diced tomatoes
1 (14-ounce) can coconut milk
1 medium head cauliflower, broken into florets
Salt and pepper, to taste

Directions
1. Heat the coconut oil in a large skillet over medium heat.
2. Sauté the onion, garlic, and ginger until softened (about 5 minutes).
3. Stir in spices until fragrant (about 1 minute).
4. Add chickpeas, tomatoes, coconut milk, and cauliflower.
5. Bring to a boil and then reduce to a simmer.
6. Cover and let simmer for 15 minutes.
7. Remove the lid and continue cooking until thickened (about 5 minutes). Season with salt and pepper to taste.

Dessert: Dutch Oven Berry Cobbler

No camping recipe book feels complete without a Dutch oven cobber, and we have not failed you! These berries are loaded with fiber, nutrients, and anti-oxidants, and they help fight inflammation.

Serves 6

Ingredients
5 cups mixed berries
1 teaspoon cinnamon
½ cup sugar
2 tablespoons cornstarch
1 ½ cups flour
⅓ cup sugar
2 teaspoons baking powder
½ teaspoon salt
5 tablespoons cold butter, cubed
½ cup 1% milk

Directions
1. To make the berry filling, combine the first 4 ingredients and mix well. Let them sit for at least an hour.
2. In a mixing bowl, combine the flour, sugar, baking powder, and salt. Cut in the butter until the mixture forms a coarse meal. Stir in the milk until a dough forms. Knead it lightly. You can choose to roll it out and cut biscuits if you like.
3. Heat a large cast iron pan over medium heat. Pour the berry mixture into the pot.
4. Spoon scoops of the dough onto the berries, or arrange your cut biscuits on top.
5. Cover the pot with a lid or tented foil.
6. Cook for about 35 minutes, until the topping is cooked.
7. Let it sit for 30 minutes before serving.

DAY TWO RECIPES

Breakfast: Vegetarian Croissant Sandwiches

Serves 4 | Method: Foil Packet

Ingredients
4 bakery croissants split in half
1 tomato, sliced
1 cup fresh spinach
1 avocado, peeled and sliced into eight wedges
4 slices provolone cheese, optional
1 teaspoon Italian seasoning

Directions
1. Packet folding style: Flat
2. Grease 4 12"x12" heavy-duty aluminum sheets.
3. Take each of the four croissants and lay one half of each in the center of a piece of aluminum foil.
4. Stack the ingredients onto the croissant, starting with the spinach, then the tomatoes, avocados, walnuts and cheese.
5. Season with Italian seasoning and black pepper before applying to the top of the croissant.
6. Create a tight, flat fold over each croissant and place on the heat source for 5-10 minutes or until the sandwich is hot and steamy.

Prep Tip: Slice and prepare the vegetables and walnuts at home before bringing to the campsite.

Lunch: Campfire Cheese and Veggies Quesadilla

Cooked over the campfire, this quesadilla makes a delicious and easy cheese-and-vegetable-packed lunch.

Serves 4

Ingredients
2 teaspoons vegetable oil
1 small red onion, finely sliced
10 button mushrooms, finely sliced
½ cup corn
Salt and pepper, to taste
4 flour tortillas
1 cup Pepper Jack cheese, grated

Directions
1. In a cast iron skillet, add oil and heat over campfire. Once oil is hot, toss in onion and mushrooms. Stir fry until tender and a bit brown. Stir in corn and cook for another few minutes. Turn off heat. Season with salt and pepper.
2. Top 4 sheets of aluminum foil with a tortilla. In a straight line along the center, place equal amounts of cheese onto each tortilla followed by the cooked vegetables. Top with another layer of cheese. Seal tortilla by folding edges to the middle, then fold aluminum foil to the center to wrap tortilla. Roll edges of foil together to secure quesadillas.
3. Place a grilling grate on top of campfire then put foil wraps on top. Cook, turning once, until cheese has melted and tortillas are crispy and toasted, about 2-4 minutes.

Supper: Dutch Oven Style Risotto

This hot and creamy rice dish combines Arborio rice with some quinoa for protein.

Serves 4

Ingredients
2 tablespoons butter
1 cup Arborio rice
½ cup quinoa
½ cup dry white wine
5 cups vegetable stock
1 cup Parmesan cheese
1 tablespoon Italian seasoning
Salt and pepper to taste

Directions
1. Prepare the Dutch oven by heating the coals and putting the oven on top of them.
2. When the oven is hot, add the butter, and let it melt. Add the Arborio rice and quinoa, and gently stir while cooking to toast the rice, approximately 3 minutes.
3. Add the white wine while continuing to stir.
4. Add the vegetable stock, stirring well, until the broth becomes hot.
5. Cover, and let cook for 25–30 minutes, or until the stock is absorbed. Stir often.
6. Add the Parmesan cheese, Italian seasoning, salt, and pepper. Stir well.

Dessert: Grilled S'mores Cones

Have this unique yet appetizing take on the classic s'mores in as quick as 15 minutes.

Serves 6 | Method: Foil packet

Ingredients
6 waffle cones
2 cups mini marshmallows
1 cup chocolate chips

Directions
1. Distribute even amounts of marshmallows and chocolate chips to each waffle cone. Then, wrap each entirely in heavy-duty aluminum foil. Secure any open edges.
2. Away from direct heat, cook on hot grill for about 7 to 10 minutes until heated through.
3. Unwrap and let cool for a few minutes before serving.

VEGETARIAN 3-DAY MENU

Day One
Breakfast: Raspberry Dutch Oven Pancake
Lunch: Zucchini Nuggets
Spicy Broccoli and Rice Bowl
Dessert: Grilled One Pan Chocolate and Berry Pound Cake

Day Two
Breakfast: Dutch Oven Eggs Baked in Avocados
Lunch: Portobello Mushroom Burger
Supper: Quinoa Stuffed Peppers
Dessert: Cookie Dough Dip

Day Three
Breakfast: Camp Quiche
Lunch: Mexican Quinoa Soup
Supper: Orange Pistachio Brown Rice
Dessert: Dreamy Chocolate Pudding

SHOPPING LIST

Fats
Butter, ¾ cup
Olive oil, ½ cup plus 2 tablespoons

Proteins

Cashews, 1 cup
Eggs, 21
Peanut butter, natural, ¼ cup
Pistachios, shelled, ¾ cup

Vegetables and fruits
Avocado, 5
Bell peppers, any color, 4
Blueberries, ½ cup
Broccoli, florets, 7 cups
Cilantro, fresh, ⅓ cup chopped
Garlic, 4 cloves
Green onions, 1 bunch
Mushrooms, 12 ounces
Onion, red, 3
Onion, white, 2
Oranges, 2
Orange juice, ¾ cup
Portobello mushrooms, large caps, 4
Raisins, sultana, ½ cup
Raspberries, 2 ½ cups
Strawberries, 1 cup
Tomato, 4
Zucchini, 1 large, 1 medium

Dairies
Cheddar cheese, shredded, 1 cup
Cream cheese, 4 ounces
Milk, 1 quart
Mozzarella, shredded, 1 cup
Swiss cheese, 4 ounces

Grains
Brown rice, 4 cups
Flour, all-purpose, 1 ⅓ cups

Hamburger buns, 4
Quinoa, 2 cups

Cans

Black beans, 1 can
Chipotle peppers in adobo sauce, 1 can
Coconut milk, 1 cup
Corn, 1 can
Vegetable stock, 3 quarts
Tomato sauce, 1 cup

Seasonings, toppings, others

Balsamic vinaigrette, ¼ cup
Chocolate bars, your choice, 2
Chocolate chips, mini, semi-sweet, 1 cup
Cocoa powder, ¼ cup
Cornstarch, 3 tablespoons
Curry powder, 2 tablespoons
Garlic salt, 1 teaspoon
Honey, 1 tablespoon
Hot sauce, 1 tablespoon
Maple syrup, ¾ cup
Pickles, sliced, 3 (optional, for portobello burger)
Pound cake, prepared, 12 ounces
Red pepper flakes
Salt
Sugar, brown, ¼ cup
Sugar, icing, ¼ cup
Sugar, white, ¾ cup
Taco seasoning, 1 tablespoon

DAY ONE RECIPES

Breakfast: Raspberry Dutch Oven Pancake

This is a quick breakfast that is delicious and easy to make. Plus, it doesn't taste at all like your usual pancake—it's way better.

Serves 6 | Method

Ingredients
6 large eggs
1 cup all-purpose flour
1 cup milk
1 teaspoon salt
2 tablespoons sugar
¼ cup butter
2 cups raspberries, divided
½ cup maple syrup, for serving

Directions
1. Prepare the fire by heating about charcoal briquettes in a chimney starter for 15 minutes or until gray.
2. As the briquettes heat up, mix the eggs and flour in a bowl. Once smooth, add in milk, salt, and sugar. Mix well until combined.
3. Take a few hot briquettes and form a ring that is just a bit smaller than the width of your Dutch oven. Lay Dutch oven on top. Melt the butter inside then spread across the bottom. Add prepared egg mixture then sprinkle 1½ cups raspberries over the mixture. Cover, then add some more hot briquettes on the lid. Cook for about 20 to 25 minutes until golden brown and set.
4. Sprinkle the rest of the raspberries on top of the pancake. Drizzle pancake syrup on top.
5. Serve.

Lunch: Zucchini Nuggets

These are a tasty way to serve zucchini that even the kids will love!

Serves 4

Ingredients
1 large zucchini
1 small red onion
⅓ cup flour
1 egg
1 teaspoon garlic salt
¼ cup butter

Directions
1. Use a cheese grater to grate the zucchini and onion. Place the vegetables on a clean kitchen towel and squeeze out as much moisture as you can.
2. Place the zucchini mixture in a bowl and add the flour egg, and garlic salt. Mix well and form it into nuggets.
3. Place a cast iron pan over medium heat and melt half the butter.
4. Fry the nuggets until they're brown on one side, then melt the remaining butter and cook them on the other side.

Spicy Broccoli and Rice Bowl

This Thai-inspired dish serves up fiber, antioxidants, and protein.

Servings: 4

Ingredients
2 quarts vegetable stock
4 cups dry brown rice
2 tablespoons olive oil, divided
6 cups broccoli florets
1 red onion, diced
8 ounces mushrooms, sliced
1 cup cashews

For the sauce:
¼ cup chipotle peppers in Adobo sauce
1 cup coconut milk
1 tablespoon honey
¼ cup natural peanut butter

Directions
1. Heat a Dutch oven over high heat and boil the stock. Stir in the rice and cook until it is softened and the liquid is absorbed.
2. Set aside half the rice for a later recipe. Keep it chilled.
3. In the Dutch oven, heat the oil and add the broccoli, red onion, and mushrooms. Stir-fry until they are crisp-tender.
4. In a bowl, combine the sauce ingredients and pour it over the vegetables. Heat until it's bubbly and hot.
5. Divide the cooked rice among the individual serving bowls. Top with the vegetable mixture and some cashews, and serve.

Dessert: Grilled One Pan Chocolate and Berry Pound Cake

This is a refreshing and simple dessert that consists of a mixture of chocolate, pound cake, and berries. Everyone's going to want seconds.

Serves 6 | Method: Grilling

Ingredients
½ cup fresh raspberries
½ cup fresh blueberries
1 cup strawberries, hulled and sliced
2 tablespoons sugar
¼ cup butter
12 ounces pound cake, cut into 1-inch cubes
2 chocolate bars of your choice, cut into small squares

Directions
1. In a bowl, combine the berries and sugar. Mix and set aside for about 10–15 minutes until the juices begin to release.
2. Heat butter in a cast iron pan over camping grill. Once melted, add pound cake pieces. Stir to make sure to evenly toasted on all sides. Remove from heat.
3. Add berries and chocolate evenly over the cake pieces. Cover with lid or aluminum foil and set aside for about 5–10 minutes to allow berries to become warm and for chocolate to melt.
4. Remove the cover and serve.

DAY TWO RECIPES

Breakfast: Dutch Oven Eggs Baked in Avocados

In this recipe, the eggs are baked in the Dutch oven in avocados to give you a creamy, healthy and rich breakfast to enjoy.

Serves 4

Ingredients
4 ripe avocados
8 eggs
Salt and pepper to taste
Red pepper flakes
Hot sauce for serving

Directions
1. Heat the Dutch oven over medium heat, about 12 coals.
2. Slice the avocados and remove the seeds. Scoop out enough of the avocado flesh as needed for the egg to fit. Lay the avocados on a flat surface.
3. Crack an egg into each avocado half.
4. Season with salt, black pepper, and red pepper.
5. Place all the filled avocados into the Dutch oven and cover it. Place 6–8 coals on top.
6. Bake for 30–40 minutes, until the eggs are done to your liking and the avocado is warmed through. Serve with a few dashes of hot sauce.

Lunch: Portobello Mushroom Burger

This burger is delicious. The crisp, cool vegetables complement the deep flavor of the mushrooms beautifully.

Serves 4

Ingredients
4 large portobello mushroom caps
¼ cup balsamic vinaigrette, your choice
4 ounces Swiss cheese
4 hamburger buns

Suggested toppings:
Sliced red onion, tomato, avocado, pickle

Directions
1. Arrange the mushroom caps on a plate. Drizzle the vinaigrette over the mushrooms. Let them sit for half an hour, turning them occasionally.
2. Heat your grill to medium and cook the mushrooms for 6–7 minutes, turning them from time to time and basting them with the marinade.
3. When they are almost done, place one ounce of Swiss cheese on each.
4. Make your burgers with your favorite toppings, and enjoy.

Supper: Quinoa Stuffed Peppers

This protein-packed meal is colorful and so tasty. You can add more or less hot sauce to customize the level of spice.

Serves 4

Ingredients
2 cups quinoa, rinsed and drained
4 cups water
2 tablespoons olive oil
1 small onion, diced
2 cloves garlic, minced
1 zucchini, diced
1 tomato, diced
½ can black beans, drained and rinsed
½ can corn kernels
1 cup tomato sauce
1 tablespoon hot sauce
Salt and pepper to taste
4 bell peppers, tops cut off and seeded
1 cup mozzarella cheese, shredded

Directions
1. Combine the quinoa and water in a saucepan and bring it to a boil. Reduce the heat and simmer until the quinoa is tender has absorbed all the water.
2. Meanwhile, in a cast iron pan, warm the oil and sauté the onion for 2-3 minutes and then add the garlic. Cook until fragrant.
3. Stir in the zucchini, tomato, beans, corn, tomato sauce, hot sauce, and salt and pepper. Set aside the remaining beans and corn for a later recipe.
4. When the quinoa is ready, set half aside for a later recipe and keep it chilled.

5. Stir the remaining quinoa into the vegetable mixture. Spoon the filling into the peppers, and top with cheese.
6. Prepare a Dutch oven over 8 coals and line it with foil. Spray the foil lightly with cooking spray.
7. Arrange the peppers in the oven and cover it with the lid. Place 12 coals on top.
8. Bake for 20–30 minutes, until the peppers are cooked to your liking and the cheese is melted.

Dessert: Cookie Dough Dip

Kids and adults alike will crowd around for this tasty dessert!

Serves 4–6

Ingredients
¼ cup butter, soft
4 ounces cream cheese, soft
¼ cup icing sugar
¼ cup brown sugar
½ cup semi-sweet mini chocolate chips

For serving
12 graham crackers
12 vanilla biscuits

Directions
1. In a medium mixing bowl, combine the butter and cream cheese together until fluffy.
2. Add the icing sugar and brown sugar, and mix to combine until it is light and fluffy.
3. Stir in the chocolate chips, and serve!

DAY THREE RECIPES

Breakfast: Camp Quiche

A perfect egg and cheese recipe that is crustless, but divine in taste.

Serves 4

Ingredients
2 tablespoons olive oil
6 eggs
1 cup broccoli, chopped
4 ounces mushrooms, sliced
1 tomato, diced
Salt and pepper to taste
1 cup cheddar, shredded

Directions
1. Whisk the eggs in a large mixing bowl, and fold in all the other ingredients EXCEPT the cheese.
2. Pour this mixture into a foil-covered pie plate.
3. Place the pie plate in the Dutch oven, cover, and place the oven over the coals or campfire (on a rack).
4. Cook 25 minutes, or until the eggs are set.
5. Just before serving, sprinkle the cheese over the quiche and let it melt.

Lunch: Mexican Quinoa Soup

Let's toss the leftover quinoa in a pot with just a few other ingredients and make a tasty and nutritious soup in minutes flat.

Serves 4

Ingredients
2 tablespoons olive oil
1 onion, diced
2 cloves garlic, chopped
2 cups cooked quinoa, left over
1 tablespoon taco seasoning
1 tomato, diced
½ can black beans, drained and rinsed
½ can corn kernels
4 cups vegetable broth
Hot sauce to taste
Salt and pepper to taste

Directions
1. In a Dutch oven over medium heat, warm the oil and sauté the onion until it begins to soften. Add the garlic and cook one more minute.
2. Add the cooked quinoa to the pot, together with the taco seasoning. Cook for 3–4 minutes, stirring occasionally.
3. Add all the remaining ingredients and cook to heat through.

Supper: Orange Pistachio Brown Rice

It doesn't sound like a camping recipe, but with only a few fresh ingredients this tart and delicious dish is so quick and simple.

Serves 4

Ingredients
2 tablespoons olive oil
4 cups cooked brown rice (left over)
½ cup sultana raisins
¾ cup orange juice
2 tablespoons curry powder
¼ cup maple syrup
¾ cup pistachios, shelled (more if desired)
1 bunch green onions, chopped
⅔ cup fresh cilantro, chopped
Salt and pepper to taste
2 oranges, sliced, for serving

Directions
1. In a large cast iron pan over medium heat, warm the oil and add the rice, raisins, orange juice, curry powder, and maple syrup. Stir to combine and cook until the mixture is hot.
2. Add the pistachios, green onions, cilantro, and salt and pepper. Cook to heat through, and serve with a few slices of fresh orange.

Dessert: Dreamy Chocolate Pudding

This pudding is so creamy and delicious, especially served warm. You can substitute other kinds of milk if you prefer.

Serves 6

Ingredients
½ cup sugar
3 tablespoons cornstarch
¼ cup cocoa powder
½ teaspoon salt
3 cups milk
½ cup mini semi-sweet chocolate chips

Directions
1. In a heavy saucepan, combine the sugar, cornstarch, cocoa, and salt. Whisk them together and gradually stir in the milk.
2. Bring it to a boil over medium-high heat, then reduce the heat and simmer for a minute or two, until thickened.
3. Remove the pot from the heat and mix in the chocolate. Stir until smooth.
4. Divide the pudding into 6 serving dishes and chill if desired.

VEGETARIAN 5-DAY CAMPING MENU

Day One
Breakfast: Eggs Benedict Casserole
Lunch: Mango Salsa Stuffed Sweet Potatoes
Supper: Mujadara (Brown Rice and Lentils)
Dessert: Foil Apple Chow

Day Two
Breakfast: Eggs with Beans and Tomatoes
Lunch: Veggie Pasta Primavera
Supper: Rainbow Chili
Dessert: No-Bake Banana Cream Pie

Day Three
Breakfast: Easy Poached Omelets
Lunch: Creamy Tomato Vegetable Soup
Supper: Curried Lentils with Quinoa
Dessert: Puff Pastry Fig Tarts

Day Four
Breakfast: Hearty Oatmeal
Lunch: Bean Salad with Jalapeño Biscuits
Supper: Black Bean Lasagna
Dessert: Mango White Chocolate S'Mores

Day Five
Breakfast: Orange Choco-nut Energy Muffins
Lunch: Quinoa "Fried Rice" with Pineapple
Supper: Vegan Stew
Dessert: Peanut Butter Cup S'mores

SHOPPING LIST

Fats
Butter, ¾ cup plus 2 tablespoons
Coconut oil, 6 tablespoons
Olive oil, ½ cup plus 3 tablespoons

Proteins
Eggs, 18
Lentils, brown, 1 cup
Lentils, red, 2 cups
Trail mix, ½ cup, ½ cup
Veggie bacon, 10 slices

Vegetables and fruits
Apples, Granny Smith, 4
Avocado, 2
Bananas, 2
Bell pepper, green, 2
Bell pepper, red, 2
Bell pepper, yellow, 3
Carrots, 2
Celery, 2 stalks
Cilantro, fresh, chopped, 1 ¾ cups
Fig preserves, 1 cup
Garlic, cloves, 11
Jalapeño peppers, 4
Lime, 2
Mango, 3
Mushrooms, cremini, 1 pound
Onion, green 2

Onion, red, 2
Onion, white, 6
Oranges, 8
Pineapple, fresh, 1
Potatoes, sweet, 4
Spinach, baby, 8 cups
Tomatoes, 3
Tomatoes, cherry, 1 cup

Dairies
Cheddar, shredded, 4 cups
Fontina cheese, 8 ounces
Half-and-half, 1 cup
Milk, 2 quarts

Grains
Chex® cereal, 2 cups
English muffins, 6
Oats, quick-cooking, 2 cups
Pancake mix, 1 ½ cups
Penne pasta, 1 pound
Quinoa, 4 cups
Rice, brown, ⅔ cup
Tortillas, corn, 6-inch, 12

Cans
Biscuit dough, refrigerated, 1
Black beans, 15-ounce can, 3
Cannellini beans, 15-ounce can, 1
Chickpeas, 15-ounce can, 2
Coconut milk, 14-ounce can, 1
Kidney beans, 14-ounce can, 1
Tomatoes, diced, 28-ounce can, 4
Tomato sauce, 8-ounce can, 4
Tomato paste, ¼ cup

Vegetable broth, 7 cups
Whipped cream, 1 can

Seasonings, toppings, others
Caramel sauce, ¼ cup
Chocolate, white chips, ½ cup
Chocolate, semi-sweet chips ½ cup
Cinnamon, ground, 3 ¼ teaspoons
Cloves, ground, ¼ teaspoon
Cumin, ground, 2 ½ teaspoons
Curry powder, 3 tablespoons
Graham crackers, 24
Instant banana pudding, 3.4-ounce package, 1
Italian seasoning, 1 tablespoon
Marshmallows, mini, 3 cups
Marshmallows, 8
Mustard, 1 teaspoon
Pepper
Puff pastry, frozen, 1 package
Red pepper flakes
Reese's Pieces® candies or Smarties®, 1 cup
Reece's Peanut Butter Cups, 8
Rosemary, dried, 1 tablespoon
Salsa, 1 ½ cups
Salt
Soy sauce, ¼ cup
Sugar, brown, 6 tablespoons
Sugar, white, ¼ cup
Taco seasoning, 3 tablespoons
Vanilla wafers, crushed, 1 cup
Vinegar, white, ¾ cup

DAY ONE RECIPES

Breakfast: Eggs Benedict Casserole

Now there is no excuse not to treat yourself to a mouthwatering breakfast when you are away camping.

Serves 4–6

Ingredients
6 English muffins, cut into small pieces
10 ounces veggie bacon, cut into pieces
6 large eggs
2 cups milk
1 teaspoon mustard
Salt and pepper to taste

Directions
1. Spray the Dutch oven with oil and set it in the coals to heat.
2. Combine the English muffin pieces with the bacon in the Dutch oven.
3. In a mixing bowl, combine the eggs, milk, mustard, salt, and pepper.
4. Pour this batter on top of the muffin and bacon mixture in the pot and jiggle the pot so it soaks in evenly.
5. Let it cook until the eggs are set.
6. Serve, and enjoy.

Lunch: Mango Salsa Stuffed Sweet Potatoes

In this recipe we combine the smooth warmth of a baked sweet potato with the crisp, lively taste of fresh mango salsa.

Serves 4

Ingredients
For the salsa
1 (15-ounce) can black beans, drained and rinsed
1 large mango, peeled and diced small
½ small red onion, diced
1 tomato, diced
1 jalapeño pepper, minced
¼ cup chopped cilantro
1 tablespoon olive oil
Juice of 1 lime

4 medium sweet potatoes

Directions
1. Prepare the salsa by combining all the ingredients. This can be done ahead of time, but it's best freshly made.
2. Wrap the sweet potatoes in foil and place them near the heat. Turn them often and cook until they're soft, 30–40 minutes.
3. Carefully open the potato packets and slice the potatoes lengthwise. Fluff the flesh with a fork and let them cool enough to eat. Serve with a helping of the salsa on top.

Supper: Mujadara (Brown Rice and Lentils)

The oldest recipe ever found for Mujadara was from the 1200s, but people say it's even older than that. It's a perfect dish to have outdoors in nature.

Serves 4

Ingredients
2 tablespoons coconut oil
1 onion, diced
3 cups vegetable broth
1 cup brown lentils
⅔ cup brown rice
½ teaspoon ground cumin
¼ teaspoon ground cloves
¼ teaspoon ground cinnamon
1 teaspoon salt
½ teaspoon red pepper flakes

Directions
1. In a Dutch oven over medium heat, melt the coconut oil and cook the onion until it is nicely colored, about 10 minutes.
2. Stir in all the other ingredients and bring the mixture to a boil.
3. Cover, and place some briquettes on the lid. You want to maintain a temperature around 325°F.
4. Cook for 45–60 minutes, checking often after half an hour, until the rice and lentils are tender and the liquid is absorbed.

Dessert: Foil Apple Chow

Serving these in individual packets helps you to control serving size. This is a good thing!

Serves 4–6

Ingredients
6 tablespoons butter
4 Granny Smith apples, cored and thinly sliced
1 teaspoon cinnamon
1 cup Reese's Pieces® candies or Smarties®
1 cup mini marshmallows
2 cups Chex cereal

Directions
1. Set out 6 12"x12" heavy-duty aluminum foil sheets and place a pat of butter on each.
2. Divide the apple slices among the foil pieces, and sprinkle with cinnamon.
3. Close the packets and place them by the heat for 3–5 minutes, until the apples have begun to soften, taking care of moving around with tongs for even cooking.
4. Carefully open the packets, and sprinkle with the other ingredients as desired. Close the foil again and return them to the heat until the marshmallows are gooey.

DAY TWO RECIPES

Breakfast: Eggs with Beans and Tomatoes

This is a savory, nutritious breakfast that is perfect for chilly mornings. It will warm you from the inside out.

Serves 4

Ingredients

2 tablespoons olive oil

½ red onion, minced

2 teaspoons cumin

½ teaspoon red pepper flakes, or to taste

Salt and pepper, to taste

1 (28-ounce) can chopped or diced tomatoes

½ (15-ounce) can cannellini beans

4 eggs

Directions

1. Heat the oil in a cast iron skillet over medium heat. Add the onion and spices and sauté until fragrant (about 1 minute).
2. Season with salt and pepper.
3. Add the tomatoes and beans. Continue cooking, with occasional stirring, until the onion is tender (about 5 minutes). Set aside the unused beans and keep them chilled.
4. Make 4 depressions in the mixture and crack an egg into each.
5. Cover and let it cook until the eggs reach the desired doneness (about 5 minutes).

Lunch: Veggie Pasta Primavera

We'll make some extra pasta today and set it aside for an even easier lunch tomorrow.

Serves 4–6

Ingredients
2 tablespoons olive oil
1 medium onion, chopped
3 cloves garlic, minced
8 ounces cremini mushrooms, sliced
1 red bell pepper, thinly sliced
½ (15-ounce) can cannellini beans
Salt and pepper to taste
1 quart vegetable broth
2 cups milk
1 pound penne pasta (small is better)
6 cups baby spinach
8 ounces fontina cheese, grated

Directions
1. Heat the oil in a Dutch oven over preheated coals. Sauté the onion and garlic until tender.
2. Add the mushrooms and cook until most of the moisture has evaporated (about 10 minutes). Add the red pepper, beans, salt, and pepper.
3. Stir in the broth and milk, and bring it to a boil. Add the pasta and stir.
4. Cover, and let it simmer until the pasta is al dente and almost all the liquid is absorbed (about 8 minutes).
5. Remove the pot from the heat and stir in the baby spinach and fontina, mixing until the cheese is melted.
6. Adjust the flavor with more salt and pepper, as needed.
7. Set side a third of the mixture and keep it chilled. Serve the remaining.

Supper: Rainbow Chili

Tonight, we're operating at peak efficiency, combining the beans and vegetables for two meals at one time. Look at us go!

Serves 4–6

Ingredients
1 green bell pepper, seeded and diced
1 red bell pepper, seeded and diced
1 yellow bell pepper, seeded and diced
2 jalapeño peppers, seeded and diced
1 red onion, diced small
2 stalks celery, diced small
1 (14-ounce) can kidney beans
1 (15-ounce) can black beans
1 (15-ounce can chickpeas

Chili
8 ounces cremini mushrooms, sliced
1 (28-ounce) can diced tomatoes
1 (8-ounce) can tomato sauce
2 tablespoons brown sugar
2 tablespoons taco seasoning
Salt and pepper to taste

Bean salad
¾ cup white vinegar
¼ cup sugar, or to taste
1 tablespoon taco seasoning
2 cups pineapple, diced small
½ cup cilantro, chopped

Directions

1. Combine the bell peppers, jalapeño peppers, red onion, celery, beans, and chickpeas in a large bowl. Mix well, and remove half the mixture to a Dutch oven.
2. Place the Dutch oven over medium heat and add the mushrooms, diced tomatoes, tomato sauce, brown sugar, chili powder, cumin, garlic powder, red pepper flakes, and salt and pepper.
3. Bring the mixture to a simmer and cook until the vegetables are softened, 30–45 minutes.
4. In a small mixing bowl, combine the remaining ingredients for the bean salad and add them to the bean mixture we set aside.
5. Mix well, and place them in a sealed bowl (or a large, reliable bag) in the cooler to marinate. Turn the bag or stir the bowl from time to time.

Dessert: No-Bake Banana Cream Pie

Comfort food by the fire. It doesn't get any better than this.

Serves 4

Ingredients
1 cup crushed vanilla wafers, divided
2 bananas, sliced
1 (3.4-ounce) package instant banana pudding
2 cups milk
Whipped cream for serving

Directions
1. Crush the vanilla wafers and divide half of them among the serving cups.
2. Place the bananas on top of the cookies.
3. Combine the pudding mix with the milk, and mix until it begins to set, and spoon it over the bananas.
4. Top with the remaining vanilla wafers, and whipped cream. Enjoy!

DAY THREE RECIPES

Breakfast: Easy Poached Omelets

The kids can customize their own baggies when you serve this fun breakfast.

Serves 4

Ingredients
8 eggs
2 cups baby spinach
1 cup cherry tomatoes, halved
2 green onions, chopped
½ yellow bell pepper, minced
1 cup cheddar cheese, shredded
Salt and pepper to taste

Directions
1. Boil 3 quarts of water in a large pot.
2. Crack two eggs into each of four resealable freezer bags. Seal the bags and shake/squeeze them gently until the eggs are lightly beaten.
3. Add your choice of ingredients and seal the bags.
4. Carefully drop the bags into the boiling water and cook for 10–12 minutes, until cooked through.
5. When they are done, an adult should remove the bags from the pot with a slotted spoon.

Lunch: Creamy Tomato Vegetable Soup

A little of this, a little of that, and nobody will recognize our leftover Pasta Primavera!

Serves 4–6

Ingredients
1 (28-ounce) can diced tomatoes
1 (8-ounce) can tomato sauce
Leftovers from Pasta Primavera
½ cup half-and-half
1–2 cups water

Directions
1. Combine the ingredients in a saucepan, mix well. Add water to the desired consistency, and heat through.
2. Sit back and enjoy!

Supper: Curried Lentils with Quinoa

This gluten-free vegan stew is very nutritious and filling.

Serves 4

Ingredients
4 cups quinoa, soaked, rinsed, and drained
7 cups water
1 teaspoon salt
2 tablespoons coconut oil
1 small onion, chopped
6 cloves garlic, minced
1 (28-ounce) can diced tomatoes
1 (14-ounce) can coconut milk
1 teaspoon cinnamon
3 tablespoons curry powder
2 cups red lentils
Salt and pepper to taste
1 cup fresh cilantro, chopped

Directions
1. In a large saucepan, combine the quinoa, water, and salt, and bring them to a boil. Reduce the heat and cook for about 15 minutes, until the quinoa is tender and the liquid is absorbed. Set half of the cooked quinoa aside for a later recipe.
2. In a large cast iron skillet over medium heat, melt the coconut oil. Sauté the onion and garlic until tender and fragrant, and then stir in the rest of the ingredients EXCEPT the cilantro.
3. Bring the mixture to a simmer and cook until the lentils are tender but not mushy.
4. Serve the lentil stew over a portion of the quinoa.

Dessert: Puff Pastry Fig Tarts

It's easy to bring along a package of puff pastry and a bottle of fig preserves for this recipe. You won't regret it!

Yields 9 squares

Ingredients
1 package puff pastry
1 tablespoon dried rosemary
4 ounces cream cheese
1 cup fig jam or preserves

Directions
1. Roll out the pastry and cut it into 9 squares. Arrange them to fit in your skillet, with the edges slightly raised to hold your filling.
2. Cut the cream cheese into 9 equal pieces and place one into each pastry cup. Sprinkle just a small pinch of rosemary onto the cream cheese.
3. Top the cream cheese with 2 tablespoons of fig jam or preserves.
4. Cover the skillet, and cook over medium heat until the pastry is cooked and the filling is hot.
5. Allow it to cool a little before serving. Enjoy!

Day Four Recipes

Breakfast: Hearty Oatmeal

This is such a wholesome and simple recipe. If you've fallen out of the oatmeal habit, this recipe will bring you back!

Serves 4

Ingredients
4 cups water
2 cups quick-cooking oats
Pinch of salt
½ teaspoon cinnamon
¼ cup brown sugar
½ cup prepared trail mix of your choice
1 cup milk
¼ cup butter

Directions
1. In a large saucepan, boil the water over high heat and add the oats, salt, and cinnamon.
2. Reduce the heat to medium low and simmer until the oats are cooked, about 5 minutes.
3. Top with brown sugar and trail mix.
4. Serve with a bit of milk and a tablespoon of butter on each bowl.

Lunch: Bean Salad with Jalapeño Biscuits

Since the bean salad is ready and waiting, let's take a little time to prepare some biscuits to go with it!

Serves 4–6

Ingredients
1 can refrigerated biscuit dough
1 jalapeño pepper, seeded and diced
¼ cup butter
1 cup cheddar cheese, shredded

Directions
1. Heat a Dutch oven over medium heat and coat it with a little of the butter.
2. Separate the biscuits and arrange them in the oven.
3. Sprinkle on the peppers and dot them with butter. Top with shredded cheese.
4. Cover and place some coals on top of the oven.
5. Bake for 20–25 minutes, until the biscuits are golden and cooked through.
6. Serve bowls of bean salad with a steamy biscuit.

Supper: Black Bean Lasagna

This is a spicy and hearty supper that everyone—vegetarians and meat lovers alike—will love.

Serves 6

Ingredients
1 tablespoon olive oil
1 onion, chopped
2 cloves garlic, chopped
½ green bell pepper, diced
½ yellow bell pepper, diced
1 ½ cups salsa
1 (15-ounce) cans black beans, drained and rinsed
Salt and pepper to taste
2 avocados, peeled, pitted, and mashed
Juice of 1 lime
12 (6-inch) corn tortillas, quartered
2 cups shredded Cheddar cheese

Directions
1. In a cast iron skillet over medium-high heat, warm the oil and sauté the onion until tender. Add the garlic and cook one more minute.
2. Stir in the peppers and cook until they begin to soften, and then add the diced tomatoes, salsa, and beans.
3. Meanwhile, mash the avocados and add the lemon juice. Mix well.
4. Place a Dutch oven over medium heat. Prepare a baking pan that will fit inside the Dutch oven and coat it with oil.
5. Spread a layer of tortillas in the baking dish. Spread on a third of the bean mixture and half the avocado. Sprinkle on a third of the cheese.

6. Add another layer of tortillas, half the remaining bean mixture, the rest of the avocado, and half the remaining cheese.
7. Add the last of the tortillas, the last of the bean mixture, and the last of the cheese.
8. Place the baking pan in the Dutch oven, cover it with the lid, and place some coals on top.
9. Bake for 30–40 minutes, until the sauce is bubbly and the cheese is melted.

Dessert: Mango White Chocolate S'Mores

Here a very sweet recipe that calls for the combination of white chocolate with tangy mango to make the most delicious dessert you could ever ask for.

Serves 8

Ingredients
½ cup white chocolate chips
8 graham crackers
2 cups mini marshmallows
¼ cup caramel sauce
1 mango, diced small

Directions
1. Line an aluminum pan with parchment paper and set it aside.
2. Break the graham crackers into squares and place half of them in the bottom of the pan.
3. Top them with the white chocolate, and then place it over warm coals until the chocolate begins to soften.
4. Remove it from the coals and top it with marshmallows.
5. Drizzle the caramel and place the blueberries on top.
6. Top with the remaining graham crackers and enjoy immediately.

DAY FIVE RECIPES

Breakfast: Orange Choco-Nut Energy Muffins

Serves 4–6

Ingredients
1 ½ cups pancake mix
½ cup dark chocolate chips
½ cup trail mix of your choice
¼ teaspoon salt
½ teaspoon cinnamon
½ cup milk
2 tablespoons coconut oil, melted
8 oranges, cut in half with insides removed

Directions
1. Packet folding style: tight wrap
2. Grease eight 6-inch squares of heavy-duty aluminum foil with cooking spray.
3. In a large bowl, combine the pancake mix, chocolate chips, trail mix, salt, and cinnamon.
4. Cut the oranges each in half, preserving any juice. Scoop out the pulp to create hollow shells.
5. Add the milk, coconut oil, and orange juice to the dry ingredients. Mix only to combine.
6. Fill one half of each orange shell with the muffin mixture. Top with the other half of the orange shell. Wrap each orange tightly in a sheet of foil.
7. Place the oranges onto heat source and cook for 15-20 minutes, turning occasionally.
8. Remove from heat and let cool 10 minutes before opening.

Lunch: Quinoa "Fried Rice" with Pineapple

This classic dish gets a nutrition makeover with quinoa and pineapple.

Serves 4–6

Ingredients
3 tablespoons olive oil
1 onion, diced
½ green pepper, diced
4 cups quinoa, left over
¼ cup soy sauce
2 cups pineapple, diced small
2 teaspoons sugar
Salt and pepper to taste

Directions
1. Heat the olive oil in a large cast iron skillet and add the onion, green pepper, and quinoa. Stir to combine.
2. When the quinoa is hot, add the soy sauce, pineapple, sugar, salt, and pepper. Cook to heat through.

Supper: Vegan Stew

This classic dish gets a nutrition makeover with quinoa and pineapple.

Serves 4–6

Ingredients
2 tablespoons olive oil
1 large onion, finely chopped
2 cloves garlic, minced
1 (15-ounce) can chickpeas, undrained
1 medium yellow bell pepper, diced
2 tomatoes, diced
2 medium carrots, peeled, diced
1 tablespoon Italian seasoning
¼ cup tomato paste
2 cups water
Salt and pepper to taste

Directions
1. Heat the Dutch oven over medium heat and warm the olive oil. Cook the onions until they are translucent, and then add the garlic.
2. When the garlic is fragrant, add the rest of the ingredients.
3. Bring the mixture to a boil, then reduce the heat and simmer for about half an hour.

Dessert: Peanut Butter Cup S'mores

Oh yes, we went there.

Serves 4

Ingredients
16 graham crackers (square)
8 peanut butter cups
8 marshmallows

You need: Sticks for roasting marshmallows

Directions
1. Set out the graham crackers and peanut butter cups within reach, placing one peanut butter cup on half the graham crackers.
2. Roast a marshmallow to your desired doneness.
3. When the marshmallow is still hot, make a sandwich by pinching the hot marshmallow between two graham crackers, with a peanut butter cup inside. Enjoy!

PRINTING THE SHOPPING LISTS

Just a quick reminder for anyone who would like to print the shopping lists. You can or find them the publisher's website www.thecookbookpublisher.com under the Authors' tab and selecting Louise Davidson's page. Just click on the document titled: Shopping Lists for 2, 3,and 5-Days Camping Trips to print them in a pdf format.

Happy camping!

RECIPE INDEX

ALSO BY LOUISE DAVIDSON

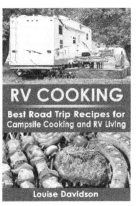  

APPENDIX

Cooking Conversion Charts

Type	Imperial	Imperial	Metric
Weight	1 dry ounce		28g
	1 pound	16 dry ounces	0.45 kg
Volume	1 teaspoon		5 ml
	1 dessert spoon	2 teaspoons	10 ml
	1 tablespoon	3 teaspoons	15 ml
	1 Australian tablespoon	4 teaspoons	20 ml
	1 fluid ounce	2 tablespoons	30 ml
	1 cup	16 tablespoons	240 ml
	1 cup	8 fluid ounces	240 ml
	1 pint	2 cups	470 ml
	1 quart	2 pints	0.95 l
	1 gallon	4 quarts	3.8 l
Length	1 inch		2.54 cm

* Numbers are rounded to the closest equivalent

Internal Temperature for Meats

Beef, Lamb, Roasts, Pork, Veal, Ham

Rare	120 – 130°F (49 – 54°C)
Medium Rare	130 – 135°F (54 – 57°C)
Medium	135 – 145°F (57 – 63°C)
Medium Well	145 – 155°F (64 – 68°C)
Well Done	155°F and greater (68°C)

Pork, ribs

Fully Cooked	190 – 205°F (88 – 96°C)

Poultry

Fully Cooked	At least 165°F (74°C)

Fish

Fully Cooked	At least 130°F (54°C)